GARDENING
from
SCRATCH
2

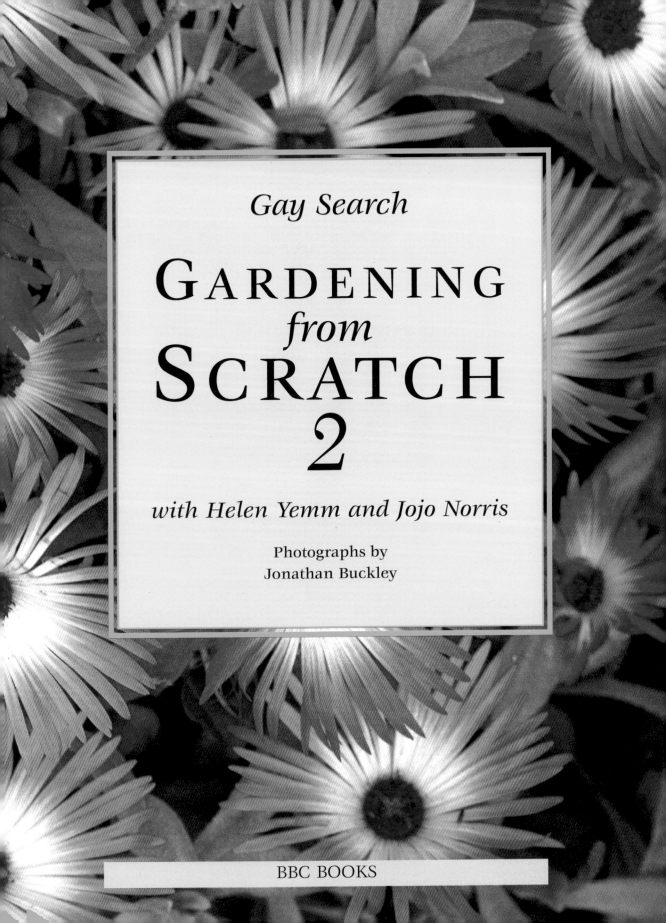

Gay Search

GARDENING
from
SCRATCH
2

with Helen Yemm and Jojo Norris

Photographs by
Jonathan Buckley

BBC BOOKS

This book is published to accompany the television series entitled *Gardening from Scratch 2* which was first broadcast in 1998. The series was produced by Catalyst Television for the BBC.

Exective Producer: Gay Search
Producer/Director: Andrew Gosling

Published by BBC Books,
an imprint of BBC Worldwide Ltd.,
80 Wood Lane
London W12 OTT.

First published 1998
© Gay Search 1998
The moral right of the author has been asserted

ISBN: 0 563 38403 4

Photographs by Jonathan Buckley © Catalyst Television
except for photograph on page 6 © Rob and Jani White

Commissioning Editor: Nicky Copeland
Project Editor: Anna Ottewill
Copy Editor: Ruth Baldwin
Designer: Sarah Amit

Typeset by BBC Books in Veljovic
Printed by Cambus Litho Limited, East Kilbride
Bound by Hunter & Foulis Limited, Edinburgh
Colour separations by Radstock Reproductions Limited, Midsomer Norton
Cover printed by Belmont Press Limited, Northampton

Contents

INTRODUCTION

Gardening, if the style sections of the newspapers and some of the glossiest magazines are to be believed, has ousted alternative comedy, football and cookery as the new rock 'n' roll. While that may be an exaggeration, it is undoubtedly true that the twenty-and thirty-somethings *en masse* no longer hold the view

Above and right: Before we started work on it, our organic garden was a typical suburban oblong with a shed that had seen better days, an area of very uneven ground under the two big gnarled apple trees and a large lawn with a very narrow border on one side.

Four months later, it looks rather different. At the far end, behind a screen of annual climbers, is a productive fruit and vegetable garden, the planting in the wider borders on both sides is filling out nicely and the uneven area under the tree, though still formal, is terraced with timber, stained a rich blue.

in using the garden as an outdoor room in which to relax and entertain friends. There is no doubt that quick, easy, cheap ideas for transforming the space with paint and other techniques borrowed from interior design and suitably adapted for the great outdoors have their place in achieving an instant effect.

At the end of the day, though, gardens are not just outside rooms. To see them only as such is to miss out on the enormous pleasure that is to be had from plants, both from looking at them and from growing them successfully, whether it's just a few in containers or lots in beds and borders. So what most beginners want, alongside good ideas and a bit of encouragement, is some basic gardening knowledge to help them get started. And that is the purpose of this book.

With *Gardening from Scratch 2* we have taken a slightly different approach. Rather than tackling a variety of topics and using our core gardens as a resource, as we did in the first television series, we have taken a more garden-based approach. Helen Yemm, who presented the first series and has taught beginners for many years, has tackled a badly neglected, not to say derelict, suburban garden in Kent, showing how, whenever possible, to work with what is already there, both in terms of structure and of plants, rather than ripping it all out and starting again with a blank canvas.

Helen's students in this garden are Gerrie (Geraldine) and Neill Lebbell. Until they bought the house a few months earlier, Gerrie had lived in flats all her life and so had never had a garden before. Neill's parents were keen gardeners, and while he took no interest in the subject in his youth, having a garden of his own for the first time made all the difference. Gerrie works, part-time now, in a leading fashion designer's London store and is prepared to be adventurous in terms of colour and form. Neill is an accountant who, while we do not wish to slip into stereotyping here, is more traditional and likes a tidy garden. They have a baby son, Evan, whose presence had to be taken in account in replanning the garden.

Our second garden is a typical suburban oblong on the outskirts of Oxford. Its owners, Jani and Rob White, were very keen to turn it into a wildlife-friendly and productive organic garden which could also accommodate their two energetic young sons, Zak, aged seven, and Finbar, aged six. Canadian-born Jani is studying to be an acupuncturist and Rob, who trained as a chartered surveyor, now works for a local housing association. Showing them the way is Jojo Norris, who has a degree in landscape architecture as well as general horticultural and organic credentials and who now works as an information officer at the main centre for organic gardening in this country, the Henry Doubleday Research Association's Ryton Gardens near Coventry.

We hope that you will be inspired by seeing what dramatic results can be achieved in a relatively short time and without spending a huge amount of money, and that, in rock 'n' roll parlance, you will go for it.

Gay Search

Acknowledgements

GRATEFUL THANKS FOR HELP WITH SUNDRIES TO:
Agralan (01285 860015) for paper mulch; Agriframes (01342 310000) for the fruit cage; Auro Organic Paints (01799 584888) for organic woodstains; BIOTAL Industrial Products Ltd (01222 747414) for the lacewing hotel; Dulux (01753 550555) for paint; Forest Fencing (01886 812451) for the gazebo; Garden Centre Trading Company (01635 42303) for the Ali-babar pot; Gloster Furniture (0117 931 5335) for the teak bench; Haemmerlin (01384 243243) for the wheelbarrow; Harcros Timber & Building Supplies Ltd (0181 337 6666); Hozelock (01844 291881) for the pump spray and pond liner; Lotus Water Garden Products Ltd (01282 420771) for pond liner, underliner, bubble pool, pump, pond repair materials; Marshalls (01422 306300) for paving; Miracle Garden Care Ltd (01483 410210) for mulches/bark etc; Pang Valley Copice Products (0181 930 5335) for peasticks/beanpoles etc; Rolawn (Turf Growers) Ltd (01904 608661) for turf; Sharpe & Fisher Building Supplies Ltd (01865 241411) for fencing; Stewart's (01844 339226) for plastic planters; Sunshine of Africa (01983 721010) for cocoa shells; TDP (01322 842685) for the Plantex membrane.

GRATEFUL THANKS FOR SEEDS AND PLANTS TO:
Chiltern Seeds (01229 581137); Ruxley Manor Garden Centre (0181 300 0084): Jim Lilley at Kennedy's Garden Centres (01344 860022); The Organic Gardening Catalogue/Chase Organics (01932 820958); Henry Doubleday Research Association at Ryton Gardens (01203 303517); Waterperry Gardens (01844 339226); Bob Collett at Petersham Nurseries (0181 940 5230).

The gardens were designed by Jojo Norris and Robin Williams and built by Michael Twite Landscapes (01789 470505) and Philip Enticknap at Landscapes by Design (01689 851570).

MY PERSONAL THANKS TO:
Gerrie and Neill, Jani and Rob, and to Helen and Jojo for their enthusiasm, their unfailing good humour – even when cold, wet and knee-deep in mud – and their willingness to get stuck in.

Finally, my very grateful thanks to the Catalyst Television production team: producer/director Andrew Gosling, production manager Matt Jones, cameraman John Couzens, sound recordist John Gilbert and to photographer Jonathan Buckley, who in addition to giving their talented, professional best as always, gave a new meaning to 'multi-skilling', pitching in to saw, dig, shift and plant when necessary to get the job done.

MAKING A START

Above: At first glance, an area like this has a rather magical quality with plants like honesty, bluebells and snow-in-summer all growing together in a delightful jumble. It's only when you look more closely that you see all the weeds growing in amongst them.

Left: It's astonishing how quickly a garden can revert to nature once it's no longer cared for on a regular basis, but the plus side with a garden like this is that once the weeds are removed, there are many mature trees and shrubs to form the 'bones' of the renovated garden.

Most of us cut our gardening teeth, as it were, not on a virgin plot behind a brand-new house but on an existing garden which could be anywhere on a sliding scale between delightful and derelict. You may be one of the lucky few who inherit the former, but even so, you will still need to learn a bit about what you have and how to look after it. If your garden is more akin to the latter, do not despair.

A derelict garden may seem an extremely daunting prospect at first sight with its broken fences, crumbling walls, cracked concrete paths, rough old tussocky grass passing itself off as a lawn, badly overgrown trees and shrubs, and the whole range of weeds from head-high brambles, docks and bindweed to, if you are really unlucky, ground elder and mare's tail. But, although it may be hard to believe, a garden like this has many advantages over a new plot or even a garden that's bare of everything except the remains of a few old bonfires, rubbish and weeds.

For a start, you have existing established trees and shrubs which give your garden invaluable structure and maturity as well as providing some privacy by screening it from the surrounding houses. You may already find, beneath the jungle, a layout to the garden which actually works very well. There may even be features – ponds, pergolas, patios – which can be repaired and brought back into serviceable use. And who knows what horticultural treasures may be concealed under that anonymous blanket of weeds?

Derelict gardens usually go with houses that have suffered almost as badly from neglect over time, and you'll probably have your work cut out – and all available cash earmarked – to get the house into a habitable state before you even look at the garden. But it's a very good idea to do just that as soon as you can – look at the garden and see what's there, even if it will be some months before you can start work on it. It is also well worth considering very early on, especially if you have moved into a terrace where the only access to the garden is through the house itself, whether it might be more sensible to do any major clearance work now when the house is a building site and you may well already have a skip outside. If you wait until the house is finished, you risk scraping the sparkling new paintwork and dirtying the nice new carpets as you cart the garden rubbish through.

The traditional advice when you take over a garden is to wait a whole year and see what comes up before you start attacking it and risk slicing through dormant plants. But obviously a lot depends on what time of year you move in. If it's in late autumn or winter, you'll get a good idea of the 'bones' – trees, shrubs, evergreens and so on – but you'll have no idea about seasonal planting, such as the bulbs, and herbaceous perennials – plants like lupins, columbines (*Aquilegia*), poppies – which disappear beneath the soil in autumn and re-emerge in spring. If you move in the spring, you'll see all the spring-flowering plants too, but still won't know what the summer will bring. Summer's probably the best time, since there'll still be remnants of the bulbs left and all the other perennials, biennials and self-sown annuals will be making their presence felt.

Make an inventory of plants

If you're a new gardener, you'll obviously recognize some plants – tulips, daffodils, roses and so on – but there'll be many others that you don't know, so ask a knowledgeable relative, friend or neighbour to walk round the garden with you and tell you what's what. It's worth taking a notebook to write down the names and as much useful information about each plant as you can: when it flowers, how big it gets, what needs doing to it to keep it growing well and so on.

Take some canes, string, plant labels and an indelible pen or pencil too, so that you can mark plants that you like and want to keep. It's also well worth marking the position of plants like bulbs and a few perennials such as bleeding heart (*Dicentra spectabilis*) whose foliage disappears by mid-summer, leaving no clue as to exactly where under the soil the dormant plant lies buried.

Trees

Next, take a careful look at the trees in your garden. They may be overgrown and look a bit of a mess, but think hard before you chop them down. For one thing, if you live in a conservation area, you won't be able to get rid of them without applying for permission from the local authority's tree officer, and there are no guarantees that it will be granted. Many local authorities won't give permission for trees to be removed unless they are dangerous or causing problems for nearby buildings. Unless your trees are real monsters and totally unsuitable for the size of your garden – sycamores, weeping willows, some conifers and limes spring to mind – think about having them pruned, thinned out and shaped so that they allow in more light and are more attractive to look at. If any major work on trees involves ladders, it isn't a good idea to do it yourself. Removing a branch 20ft above the ground with no risk to life, limb or next door's greenhouse is quite an art. So always use a properly qualified tree surgeon – your local authority's tree officer will probably have a list of recommended ones – and never allow a cowboy with a chainsaw who knocks, uninvited, on your door to touch your trees.

Shrubs

Now take a look at your shrubs. These are likely to include at least some of the larger usual suspects – winter-flowering jasmine, flowering currant, forsythia, lilac – which, to be honest, are not ideal small garden shrubs since they flower attractively enough for a few weeks each year and then remain rather dull for the rest of it. But, again, before you chop, think about the function they are fulfilling – screening out an unattractive view at the bottom of the garden, perhaps, or providing some privacy from the neighbours. In that case, prune them to reduce their size and remove the old and dead wood to encourage healthy new growth. To brighten them up, you could plant a small late-flowering clematis, such as *Clematis viticella* or *C. texensis* to scramble through them. These clematis flower from July onwards, giving you a second show in the same space, and since they can be cut right back to within a few centimetres of the ground in late autumn, they don't interfere with the shrub when it's giving its own show in spring or early summer.

Once any new shrubs you plant are big enough, you can take the old ones out if you want to. Some shrubs which are shallow-rooted, such as heathers, hebes and cotton lavender, may just be in the wrong place and can be moved successfully, though it's best done between late autumn and early spring when they are dormant.

Another way to treat big old shrubs is to use them as hedging plants. You might as well wait until flowering is over – that's their main charm, after all – then prune them with loppers or secateurs to reduce the size, after which you can clip them with shears more or less square, just as you would any hedge.

> ❛ As soon as you can, look at the garden and see what's there, even if it will be some months before you can start work on it ❜

Where to start

Where you start will depend on just how badly overgrown your garden is. If it really is covered in weeds, it makes sense to cut them back enough to see what there is underneath so that you can decide which plants you would like to save.

It's relatively simple to work round trees and shrubs while you clear the ground because they have woody stems and are much taller than the weeds, but it's much more difficult with perennials which have soft stems and are often tangled up with the weeds. So the logical first step is to create a holding bed for the perennials you want to save while you sort out the rest of the garden.

Choose a shady spot if possible, where the plants are less likely to dry out (they do need to be kept moist), and simply strip off the top layer of weeds. Dig the bed over, removing every piece of weed root you can find. In a garden neglected for many years, weeds will be a major problem for some time, so take every opportunity to remove them where you can.

Perennial plants are easy to move at any time of year, even when they are in full flower, as long as you water them thoroughly.

1 Soak the plant you are going to dig up – a bucketful of water poured slowly on to to a large clump is about right – and then dig the hole in the holding bed ready to receive it.
2 Dig carefully right round the plant about 15cm (6in) from it, keeping the spade as vertical as possible, and once it feels loose slide the spade underneath and carefully lever the rootball up. If you feel any resistance, that means some of the roots are still in the soil, so dig a little deeper and try again.

3 Once you have lifted the clump, carefully pull out all the weeds you can see growing around and through it. Take out, too, any roots you see that are clearly different from those firmly attached to the plant, since they are likely to be weeds.

4 If the soil is very dry, fill the planting hole with water before you put the plant in it.

5 Put the plant in the hole, half-fill around it with dry soil and water again.

6 Complete the filling with dry soil, sealing all the moisture in. That way the water will stay where you want it – round the roots of the plant – and it won't evaporate wastefully into the air.

7 If there is lots of top growth on the plant, cut it back by about half to prevent the plant losing moisture through its leaves.

8 Label all the plants that you've saved and check the holding bed frequently to make sure that the plants never dry out.

When you are ready to replace the plants in their permanent positions in the prepared, weed-free soil, water them well first, dig them up carefully – they should come out much more easily this time, since they won't have had so long to get their roots down – and put them straight into the new planting holes. Water thoroughly once more, and keep an eye on them until they are growing well.

Saving seedlings

It is also well worth hunting out seedlings of biennials like foxgloves and honesty and saving them in your holding bed. These are plants that grow one year, flower the next and then die. Any biennial plants that are currently flowering or are about to flower will die at the end of the summer, but nearby you are likely to find lots of seedlings, easily recognizable by the leaves (the same as the parents'), which will flower next year. There are a few exceptions, though: for

Right: One of the joys of taking on a derelict garden is that you inherit some bold plant combinations which you would not have considered yourself. Orange alstroemeria and mauve everlasting pea shouldn't work together, but they do.

Above: A few plants such as this rich red paeony do not like being moved so, if you want to keep them, leave them where they are and plant around them.

example, the seedlings of wild alconet (a real garden thug which needs to be removed from your garden, not saved) look very similar to those of foxgloves. The good news is that they are very different to the touch – the former's leaves are bristly while the latter's are smooth and velvety.

Treat seedlings in the same way as the larger plants you've saved (see pages 13–14).

Getting rid of weeds

Undoubtedly the best way to get rid of all but the most pernicious perennial weeds (those that come back year after year) is by digging, hoeing or hand-weeding. The secret, Helen Yemm maintains, is to take only a small area at a time and do it properly, rather than having a go at a larger area and leaving half the weeds behind.

Where there are just a few well-spaced plants or no plants at all, you can use a hoe to get rid of annual weeds. Always walk backwards as you work, leaving the weeds on the surface to shrivel up and die. If you work the other way, you may well tread on the weeds you have hoed out and inadvertently heel them back into the soil again.

Where there is dense planting, use a small hand fork to loosen the soil, then pull out every little weed, roots and all. As you work collect them in a bucket and then dump the whole lot. Some weeds such as dandelions have very deep taproots and unless you get out every bit the weeds will regrow. The same applies to oxalis, which grows from tiny bulbs. Unless you remove them all it will come back.

Never let weeds flower or set seed. The old saying 'One year's seeds are seven years' weeds'

> ❛ *Never let weeds flower or set seed. The old saying "One year's seeds are seven years' weeds" isn't far from the truth* ❜

isn't far from the truth. A single dandelion clock contains thousands of seeds and even if only a tiny percentage of them germinates, you can see you will have a major dandelion problem.

For the real garden thugs – ground elder, bindweed and so on – digging cannot always solve the problem. Bindweed is such a menace because it will regrow from even a millimetre of root left in the soil, and if it is growing through established plants you want to keep, digging isn't an option anyway. If time is not of the essence, and you have a large area to deal with, excluding all light from the weeds is the best way of killing them. It's also a good way of improving the soil, because while these weeds are a menace alive, when dead they break down like all other plants and become valuable organic matter in the soil. Use sheets of thick black polythene or, if you have any, old carpet, weighted down at the edges with bricks or stones or even soil, so that all light is excluded. It will take a year for the weeds to die completely, and your garden won't look very attractive during that time, but bear with it and explain to your neighbours that it is only a temporary measure.

Chemical control

If you want to garden organically, there are no acceptable chemical weedkillers you can use. In the past, some gardeners who considered themselves organic have used weedkillers based on glyphosate since it does not persist in the soil and appeared to be completely safe for soil organisms, wildlife and humans. New evidence from the USA, however, suggests that it has some minor adverse effects on beneficial creatures and soil organisms, which rules it out for people who wish to be wholly organic in their approach.

For non-organic gardeners, though, it remains the most efficient weedkiller there is. Unlike some weedkillers which kill off only the top growth, it kills the weed right down to its roots, and unlike other weed-killers which persist in the soil for some months, once the weeds are dead and have been removed it is safe to replant right away.

If you have a large area to tackle, hire or borrow a pressure sprayer because that produces the very fine droplets you want. They adhere much better to the leaves and stems than large drops from a watering can and are absorbed more efficiently by the weeds. Don't be tempted to slosh it on, on the basis that if a little kills the weeds, a lot will kill them even more efficiently. It won't. It will simply run off and not do the job as well.

If a whole patch is derelict, you can simply spray everything. If you have shrubs or trees worth saving among the weeds, though, it is slightly more complicated. If possible, pull the weed growth clear of the plants and shield them with a sheet of cardboard or hardboard while you spray. If they are right in among the weeds, cover those you want to keep with polythene dustbin bags and then spray the weeds. Leave

6 Keep a close eye on the weeds and pull them out when they are very small. It's only once they are established that they cause real problems. 9

the bags in place until the weedkiller is completely dry, because it will kill any plant with which it comes into contact.

Once the ground is clear of weeds, keep it that way as far as possible by mulching – spreading a thick layer of organic matter such as bark, compost or cocoa shells or even a layer of gravel over the soil. A planting membrane, as tough as you can find, will also help here, though as it isn't very attractive to look at you will need to cover it with just a thin, cosmetic layer of another form of mulch. While it will keep most weeds at bay, the real thugs such as bindweed which can even push through concrete may still emerge. Treat the new growth with glyphosate when it is growing strongly in spring or summer. It may take several goes but eventually it will die. In any neglected garden, weeds will continue to be a problem for some time, since weed seeds can survive many years in the soil before they germinate, so plant accordingly. Shrubs and perennials can cope well enough, but if you want to grow annuals, which is undoubtedly the cheapest way to fill space, plant them out as young plants rather than sowing seed direct into the soil. Keep a close eye on the weeds and pull them out when they are very small. It's only once they are established that they cause real problems.

A DERELICT GARDEN

Our derelict garden was about 30m (100ft) long and 6m (20ft) wide and faced north-west. The house had originally been owned by an architect and the garden had been laid out and planted with some care. It was divided into four areas or 'rooms', the ideal design solution for a long narrow garden. First there was a cement crazy-paving patio, dominated by a large circular concrete pool full of sludge, a few irises and a struggling water lily, dozens of frogs and a zillion tadpoles. There was a large straggly hydrangea right outside the back door, a self-seeded cherry growing in the narrow border to the right along with a mixture of herbaceous plants, small shrubs and weeds, and a huge rambling rose growing up the wall of the garage on the left.

Above and right: By midsummer, only four months after we started work on it, our derelict garden looks anything but. The rustic screens and densely planted borders give it a cottage garden feel and the final step – the newly turfed lawn – sets it all off to perfection.

Left and left above: The recycled patio. The old broken concrete looks terrific reused as crazy paving within diamonds of brick and the derelict pond really has taken on a new lease of life as a bog garden and safe water feature.

At the far end of the garage was a curious brick-built tank, with a galvanized – and leaky – metal water tank balanced on top of it.

The second area, up a few steps between crumbling 'rockery' walls made from lumps of concrete, was a reasonably large-sized area of rough weed-filled grass with borders on each side.

On the south-west-facing side there was a huge cherry tree bearing two very different sorts of flowers – double pink ones and small single white ones. It had escaped from its graft many years ago, so that now it was a mixture of the cultivated ornamental variety producing double pink flowers and the wild cherry, on to the rootstock of which the ornamental one had been grafted, bearing the single white.

There were also a hawthorn, forsythia and lots of different roses in a variety of sizes, including bushes where the suckers had more or less taken over the cultivated variety. There was also a large japonica (*Chaenomeles*) with orange flowers, several huge gnarled buddleias, lots of columbines, a few oriental poppies, alstroemeria, snow-in-summer (*Cerastium tomentosum*), foxgloves, tulips, honesty and a wide range of weeds such as goosegrass, dandelions, oxalis, brambles and so on. Across the garden at the end of this area there were two deep beds, narrowing to a path between two rose bushes which, despite the disparity in size, seemed to be a pair.

The path led to the third section, which was primarily a huge mound covered in weeds. We feared it might conceal an air-raid shelter, which would have been seriously bad news since they were built to resist all attempts to demolish them and continue to do so. In the event it turned out to be nothing more sinister than many years of garden rubbish piled up in a heap.

The fourth section was dense woodland – some sort of thorn, a purple-leafed plum, conifers and large shrubs such as philadelphus and lilac.

In April when we first saw the garden, for all its dereliction it did have a rather magical atmosphere, which, as Helen said, we should try hard to preserve. There's always a danger when you renovate an old garden that you strip away everything, including the intangible quality that drew you to it in the first place.

The trick is to try to preserve the mood of the garden where possible by incorporating design ideas that are in sympathy with the elements you want to keep. Obviously 'what is already there' is the key. If it's dreadful, starting more or less from scratch is the best option. If it's merely dull – just a rectangle of lawn with narrow borders round the edge, for instance – you can make a big difference very quickly, easily and cheaply by reshaping the lawn, and creating larger borders in the process.

We were lucky in that the layout of our derelict garden basically worked very well. The patio was large enough and in the most obvious place. If you were starting afresh, you wouldn't put quite such a large pond in the middle of it, but overall it was more of an asset than a liability. The hydrangea and the cherry had to go, and other shrubs were pruned back and fed.

Since Gerrie and Neill had spent practically every penny on the house itself, designer Robin Williams suggested reusing the concrete crazy paving but making the whole patio look far more stylish by using pieces of it within large diamonds of brick . Once the bricks were down, pieces of crazy paving were laid within each diamond, set quite widely apart with broad bands of mortar in between. It worked extremely well, and certainly didn't have the 'brand-new' look we were keen to avoid.

A circle of the same bricks was laid around the pool and across the bottom of the steps up to the lawn area and they were also used to face the existing wall of the raised bed to give the patio area a greater sense of unity.

The second part of the garden remained largely the same, with grass – to call it a lawn would leave us vulnerable under the Trades Descriptions Act – and with the borders increased in size.

When you are working on an old garden, the lawn takes such a bashing with feet, wheel-barrows and piles of rubbish being dragged across it that it makes sense to tackle it last. We planned to try to salvage it, by cutting it regularly, weeding and feeding it. Even edging a rough old lawn neatly can make all the difference. In fact, if you have only half an hour to im-prove a garden's appearance, edge the lawn rather than mow it or weed the borders, as a neatly edged lawn creates the immediate impression that someone cares!

We added a path of slabs laid in the grass around the edge, leading to the seat by the west-facing border and round to the arch. There was an argument for making the path follow the shortest route straight through the middle of the grass, but we felt it would reduce the playing area and make the lawn simply a thoroughfare. Some of the foot traffic would use the path and some would cut across the lawn, but it wouldn't create too much wear and tear.

That part of the garden was very exposed to the neigh-bouring gardens, particularly on the north-east-facing side where there was just a low, squared-trellis fence. So as a cheap, quick, temporary measure we stapled lengths of 1.5m- (5ft)-high, lightweight, split-bamboo screening to the existing fence posts. It's not a solid barrier – you can still see light and

---

Shrubs which can be given a new lease of life

Prune hard to near-ground level in early spring:

Butterfly bush
(*Buddleia*)

Dogwood
(*Cornus alba*)

Hardy fuchsia

Golden or
purple-leafed elder
(*Sambucus*)

Purple-leafed smoke bush
(*Cotinus coggygria*)

White willow
(*Salix alba*)

Lavatera

Prune hard after flowering:

Mock orange
(*Philadelphus*)

Forsythia

Lilac
(*Syringa*)

Weigela

Flowering currant
(*Ribes sanguineum*)

Deutzia

---

shapes through it – so it doesn't feel claustrophobic. You can see over it, too, but at least when you're sitting in the garden you are below eye level and therefore you get the feeling of privacy.

A sense of privacy in the garden is almost more impor-tant than the real thing. A pergola, for example, if you are overlooked, does not make you invisible to the watching world, but it creates the impression of a screen, a barrier between you and it. So, as a more permanent boundary, we erected a rustic screen, about 2m (6½ft) high with uprights about 2m (6½ft) apart, along that side of the garden, in front of the split bamboo, up which we grew climbing roses and both the early and late Dutch honey-suckles (*Lonicera periclymenum* 'Belgica' and *L. p.* 'Serotina'). Again, it's by no means a solid barrier, but it creates an illusion of enclosure.

We carried the rustic screens round, across the garden at the back of the two beds, with an arch over the path, to complete the sense of enclosure. Once we had cleared the huge pile of rubbish – many hands and lots of trips to the skip outside – and had pruned one or two of the larger shrubs back quite hard, we were left with a good space, fringed by trees and shrubs and quite separate from the rest of the garden. A secret garden, entered via a narrow path under

Far left and left: The old fence provided very little privacy, so we put up very inexpensive split-bamboo screening as a short-term measure. In front of it, we planted climbing roses and honeysuckle up the new rustic screen which will eventually create the all-important feeling of enclosure.

Left: Raking in the fertilizer just before turfing is also a final opportunity to remove any stones and level out small dips and bumps.

Right: Always work from a scaffolding plank when you are laying turf, and butt up the joints very closely together.

Left: Make sure the end of the bamboo screening is absolutely vertical, otherwise the top will not be straight.

Below: Attach it to the fence posts with galvanized staples. You'll need at least one every 30 centimetres to hold it firmly in position.

the new arch, suggested itself, quite different in mood from the rest of the garden. We left the woodland area alone, apart from a bit of medicinal pruning. It provides a useful hidden space for compost heaps and for storage, and will be a wonderfully mysterious place for the Lebbels' young son to explore when he is older.

By dividing a long narrow garden like this one into separate 'rooms' and particularly by enclosing spaces and then opening them up again, you make it appear much larger than it is, and because you can see only a section at a time, you are lured further into the garden to explore. Creating focal points to draw the eye is another way of inviting people to explore further, but use them with care. In a small garden you really need only one or two, sited well away from each other, or else the eye is confused and doesn't know where to look. Try not to create too much visual clutter. The rustic screens across the garden, for instance, were built to be lower than the planting in front of them so that you would see the roof of the gazebo above the soft outlines of the planting without another strong horizontal line cutting through the picture.

New plants to complement existing ones

Where you already have mature plants in the garden, it makes sense to use them as the basis for your colour scheme. It also makes life easier for new gardeners to work a small area at a time, rather than tackle a whole border, and if you wind up with clashing colour schemes adjoining, you can simply plant some neutral white flowers or foliage shrubs to provide a visual buffer zone.

Since we had inherited lots of roses, we waited until they started flowering and we could see what colour they were and then chose plants to complement them. Around strong pink roses, for instance, we planted blue hardy geraniums, the white Californian tree poppy (*Romneya coulteri*)

and blue *Ceratostigma willmottianum*.

Bear in mind that the dominant colour in an area can change with the seasons. The large japonica (*Chaenomeles*) in our garden was brilliant orange, but flowered in spring and was over by the time the bright mauve everlasting pea (*Lathyrus*) growing through it was in bloom. Orange alstroemeria growing up through the japonica flowered in midsummer too, but it was a softer orange that worked very well with the mauve of the pea. So for permanent planting on the screens behind we chose the soft yellow-and-pink early Dutch honeysuckle (*Lonicera periclymenum* 'Belgica') and the cream-centred, red and purple petalled late Dutch honeysuckle (*L. p.* 'Serotina') which would accommodate both tones, along with white and very pale pink climbing roses, 'Madame Alfred Carrière' and 'The New Dawn' respectively.

For summer bedding to fill in the gaps for this year, we took the colour of the pea as our theme and went for pink and white lavatera (*Lavatera trimestris* 'Silver Cup' and 'Mont Blanc'), white, pink and mauve cosmos and scented white tobacco plants (*Nicotiana affinis*).

Returfing a lawn

Having fought the good fight with the grass in the derelict garden, we finally had to admit defeat. With the rest of the garden looking very good, it really needed a decent lawn to set it off to perfection, and the existing one still looked scruffy, with more of the coarser grasses and weeds than the finer grasses we needed. We wanted an instant effect so we chose to turf it rather than sow it from seed. This method is more expensive but the effect is instant and you can start using it that much sooner than you can a lawn from seed.

Whether you use seed or turf, all but the final stages are the same. Although you may be dying to get to the fun part of the job, thorough preparation is essential. You can lay turf any time of year, but you make life much easier for yourself if you do it in autumn or spring when there is likely to be plenty of moisture about. If you do need to lay it in summer, make sure the turf never dries out until it has rooted and is growing strongly, otherwise it will shrink and leave ugly gaps.

If you have an existing lawn, start by killing it off with a glyphosate weedkiller. Once the grass is dead, you can either skim off the top layer of dead vegetation and dump it, or you can dig it over, chopping it up finely with a spade, so that it goes back into the soil as organic matter. In our garden, to avoid activating the zillion weed seeds in the soil, we didn't dig it over, but simply roughed up the top inch or so with the rake.

The next stage is to level the soil with a rake, sorting out any obvious hills and valleys and removing any weed roots or large stones you come across. After this it is essential to make a good, level base and to do this you can either adopt Helen's method of dragging a plank, weighted with bricks or stones, over the surface, or you can do it the more traditional way by walking over every inch of the soil, with your weight on your heels, to compact it thoroughly. A roller simply won't do the job as well because while it will flatten the hills it misses the valleys.

Add fertilizer – blood, fish and bone, if you want to be organic, or Growmore – at the rate recommended on the packet, and then rake over the surface lightly to work it in. This also helps to loosen up the soil to make a hospitable base for either turf or seed. This is also the last chance to get rid of any small dips or ridges, so squat down every few metres and look along the surface, just to make sure that it is as level as possible.

If the weather has been very dry, put the sprinkler on for a few hours the evening before you plan to turf so that the surface is just moist. Buy the best quality turf you can afford from a reputable firm and choose a grade suitable for your needs. Obviously, if it's for a family garden, you need something that can stand up to a bit of wear and tear. If it's a bowling green look you're after, then go for the very finest grade. Order it to be delivered the day before you plan to lay it. You'll also need a scaffolding plank to work from.

On a square or rectangular lawn, start at one corner and lay the first roll along a straight side. If you need to join it, make sure the join isn't too close to a corner because that leaves the short end vulnerable to damage. Ensure the turves are butted up tightly against each other, and never stretch them to make them fit or they will shrink and leave gaps. Then bang down the turf with the back of a rake to make sure the roots are in close contact with the soil.

Working from the scaffolding plank laid on the first row of turf, lay the second staggering the joins like bricks in a wall. Once they are laid, use the back of the rake to pull the turves in the second row snugly up against the first row. Carry on until the whole area is covered.

If you have a curved lawn, then lay turf right round the edge first, cutting small wedge-shaped pieces out to accommodate concave curves and using them to fill in the convex ones. Once done, fill in with straight rows. To ensure that any joins fit neatly, lay the edge of the new turf over the turf already laid round the edge, locate the join with the knife and using the edge of the laid turf as a guide, cut through the overlying turf.

Keep making sure your newly laid turf never dries out and once the grass and has taken on a fresh green colour, you'll know that it has rooted. Once it is growing strongly, you can start mowing with the mower blades on the highest setting to start with. Lower them for subsequent cuttings, but in times of drought it pays dividends to leave the grass longer – at least 2.5cm (1in) in length.

AN ORGANIC GARDEN

More and more people, particularly younger people, are becoming interested in organic gardening. For some of them it is all part of an increasing awareness of green issues and a more holistic approach to life in general. As the German poet and philosopher Goethe wrote around two hundred years ago, 'Nothing happens in living nature that is not in relation to the whole.'

There is a growing interest in wildlife too. With agribusiness taking over the countryside and intensive farming methods depriving many of our native creatures of their habitats, private gardens are becoming increasingly important as alternative havens, and not just country gardens either. Even inner city gardens, especially those near railway lines which act as corridors for wildlife, play host to squirrels, foxes, frogs and toads, as well as to birds. Apart from the altruism of doing your bit for the planet, there are also benefits that come from encouraging butterflies and birds into your garden, and from having toads and

Above left: Looking back at the house from our organic garden, it was obvious that the area of rough tussocky grass and mud outside the back door was the ideal place for a patio that could be used all year round. Left: To link the patio with the rest of the garden, and give it a softer organic feel, we used the same timber, stained blue, as we had used around the tree and for the path to make a grid pattern on the patio.

Above: Painting the fence, and next door's extension wall the same rich cream colour as the house immediately gave the area a unity that it had lacked before. Changing the dull green paint of the woodwork to bright yellow and rich blue also gave the area a sunny Mediterranean feel.

frogs around to eat the forms of wildlife – slugs, snails and other pests – which aren't so welcome.

For other people the route to organic gardening is through their stomachs. They no longer want to eat fruit and vegetables that are sprayed with endless chemicals to protect them from pests and diseases (on average we consume 4.5 litres [1 gallon] of pesticides each per year!), to enhance growth, to retard growth, to preserve them on their long journey to the consumer (often half-way round the world) and to extend their supermarket shelf life. These people want to grow their own produce, to know exactly what they are eating and to experience the delights of consuming food that was growing in the ground twenty minutes, not twenty days, earlier.

Certainly that was Jani and Rob White's main motive. They were already part of a co-operative buying organic produce and so were very keen to learn how to grow their own. They were also keen to do something with the rest of the garden to give them somewhere tranquil and beautiful to sit as well as a safe place for their sons to play.

Jani's and Rob's garden – roughly 24m (80ft) long and 6m (20ft) wide and facing just south of east – was ideal to get across the message that anyone can create an organic garden, no matter where they live. You don't need a small-

Plants to attract birds
Snowy mespilus (*Amelanchier*)
Elder (*Sambucus*)
Rowan or Mountain ash (*Sorbus*)
Hawthorn (*Crataegus monogyna*)
Holly (*Ilex*)
Berberis
Cotoneaster
Spindle (*Euonymus europaeus*)
Firethorn (*Pyracantha*)
Michaelmas daisy (*Aster*)
Honesty (*Luneria annua*)
Evening Primrose (*Oenothera*)
Cornflower (*Centaurea cyanus*)
Sunflower (*Helianthus annuus*)

holding in the heart of the country or masses of space. The garden of the average suburban semi or the small estate town house will do just as well.

The advantages of organic gardening

For many people, organic gardening still has a faintly hippie image – sandals, piles of old tyres, small, scabby, gnarled vegetables, weeds allowed to flourish – but 'organic' does not mean scruffy and overgrown with borders full of stinging nettles and nothing but native plants bearing insignificant, rather dull little flowers. You can have a lovely garden that is a pleasure to be in, filled with colourful ornamental plants which will attract all the birds, bees and butterflies you could want. You can grow wonderful produce that not only does you no harm but has also been shown to be much more nutritious than the shop-bought, non-organically grown equivalent.

In organic gardening you use no weedkillers or artificial fertilizers. You use only plant-based insecticides, which do not get into the food chain, and which are permitted as a very last resort. You feed the soil, not the plants, with compost or well-rotted manure. You control pests and diseases by choosing, where possible, plants that are resistant to disease, by growing them 'hard', not soft and sappy, and by including plants which will attract natural predators of common pests – ladybirds and hoverflies to feast on aphids, thrushes to eat the snails, and so on.

The previous owner of Jani's and Rob's garden had used no chemicals on it for forty years, but even if you inherit a garden which has had chemicals poured all over it in recent years, it doesn't matter – you can still start to garden organically straight away. Equally the previous owner of their garden had added nothing to the heavy clay soil either in that time, so it was a bit low on nutrients, and in its natural state, either baked like concrete when it was dry or was sticky enough for making pots when it was wet! In organic gardening, the structure of the soil is disturbed as little as possible, but it's worth working organic matter, like well-rotted compost, into such heavy soil before you plant to improve the drainage.

Redesigning the garden

The main features of the garden were two large old apple trees about a third of the way down, forming a natural screen across it as well as providing support for a hammock and the

Plants to attract bees and butterflies
Michaelmas daisy (*Aster*)
Butterfly bush (*Buddleia davidii*)
Pot marigold (*Calendula*)
Valerian (*Centranthus ruber*)
Hebe
Lavender
Phlox
Scabious
Iceplant (*Sedum spectabile*)
Feverfew (*Tanacetum parthenium*)
Thyme
Rosemary
Golden rod (*Solidago*)
Sweet William (*Dianthus barbatus*)
Candytuft (*Iberis*)
Wallflower (*Cheiranthus cheiri*)

most wonderful natural climbing frame for the children. The ground beneath them was decidedly uneven with a difference of 60cm (2ft) or more in height. Between the house and the apple trees was an area of uneven tussocky grass enclosed by the concrete-block garage wall on one side and the neighbours' extension and a larch-lap fence on the other – the obvious place for a patio.

Beyond the garage was a nice old shed in need of a lick of paint, and a pile of logs left deliberately as a haven for wildlife and christened Frog Hilton. On the other side of the apple trees was a lawn in good shape with a very narrow border along the south-facing side and, at the far end, a damson tree, a small green metal shed, concrete hard standing and various structures, function unknown, made from breeze blocks.

As well as being an experienced organic gardener, Jojo Norris originally qualified as a landscape architect and also works as a garden designer, so she applied her skills to Jani's and Rob's garden. In design terms it made sense to turn the third at the far end into a fruit and vegetable plot, complete with fruit cage and compost bins. Raised beds were ideal here because raising the soil would help the drainage of the heavy clay, and edging them with timber made the vegetable plot look attractive as

Left and below: Any patio benefits greatly from plenty of well-planted containers, and choosing a very simple, strong colour scheme, not only for the plants but also for the containers themselves, creates immediate impact.

We painted inexpensive plastic planters, suitably undercoated with an acrylic primer, with the same gloss paint as we had used on the woodwork, and chose blue and yellow plants, such as Osteospermum *'Buttermilk'* (top left), Argyranthemum *'Jamaica Primrose'*, Felicias, lobelia and *yellow trailing* Helichrysum petiolatum 'Aureum'.

Above: The rich egg-yolk yellow climbing rose 'Dreaming Spires' was the perfect choice to grow over the newly painted blue shed, especially in an Oxford garden.

Below: In our containers, we used organic compost which is becoming more widely available in garden centres. We planted blue lobelia along with a new container plant Anagallis 'Skylover' which has flowers of a stunning intense blue.

well as functional. We used tannalized timber, which is pressure-treated with chemicals to prevent it rotting for up to twenty-five years. Some organic gardeners would not use treated timber because of the chemicals and would be prepared to replace untreated timber every five to ten years when it rotted. Others take the view that properly tannalized timber is 100 per cent safe and does not leach any chemicals into the soil.

We stained the wood in the vegetable garden – the edging and the compost bins – with a rich blue, organic, plant-friendly woodstain. We decided to screen off the fruit and vegetable garden with something decorative and edible, so we chose espalier fruit trees – different varieties of pear – trained against wire supports across the garden on either side of a central arch, which would be covered with the wonderful ornamental gourd 'Turk's Turban'. Since autumn is the best time to plant trained fruit, we decided to grow annual climbers such as asarina and morning glories, runner beans and edible gourds as a temporary measure for the summer.

In the middle part of the garden we kept the lawn, but removed the concrete path on the south-facing side and made the existing border much wider. To enclose the lawn we also dug out a new, narrower border on the north-facing side of the garden. We brought both borders into the middle of the garden at the entrance to the lawn area by the apple trees and again at the far end, in front of the screen, ending at the central arch.

We also put in a narrow, elong-ated kidney-shaped wildlife pond in the corner created by the screen and the south-facing border – ideally placed

> 6 *Some organic gardeners would not use treated timber and would be prepared to replace untreated timber every five to ten years. Others take the view that tannalized timber is 100 per cent safe* 9

to encourage frogs and toads to go pest-hunting in the vegetable garden, while the relocated Frog Hilton behind the pond would provide shelter for them and for hedgehogs.

To improve the uneven terrain under the apple trees we built shallow retaining walls with large chunks of 15 x 15cm (6 x 6in) timber. The aim was to maintain the difference in levels but at the same time hold the soil in place. We used the same timber to form a stepping-stone path through to the lawn. It was originally grass, but like any narrow area that takes a lot of traffic it had become very bare. With chunks of timber laid at comfortable stride-long intervals to take some of the wear and tear, turf laid in the gaps would maintain an impression of grass.

To carry through the informal feel of the rest of the garden to the patio we used the same chunky timbers as a grid, framing squares of textured honey-coloured concrete paving. Again, we used tannalized timber – the only realistic option where it is part of a construction – and stained it the same rich blue. To accommodate the slope from north to south on the patio, we levelled the main area and created a ramp to the back gate and a raised bed, made from chunky timber, along the garage wall.

We painted that wall, the neighbours' extension and the fence the same colour as the house – magnolia – which immediately made the space look bigger and gave it a unity. The woodwork on the house and garage was painted blue and yellow, while the old shed was repaired to make it weatherproof, then sanded down and also painted a rich blue. Over it we planted a yellow climbing rose, 'Dreaming Spires', an appropriate choice since the garden is in Oxford.

Planting the containers

As the green woodwork on the back of the house was painted yellow and blue while we were working on the garden, we took blue and yellow as our theme for the patio pots. Certainly colour co-ordinating containers and plants creates enormous impact. Cheap and simple square and round ribbed-plastic containers in different sizes were treated with an acrylic undercoat and then painted with either the same blue gloss as the shed, or the same yellow as the house woodwork. Blue and yellow plants were chosen to go in them: chalky blue felicias and ageratums, rich blue *Salvia farinacea* and trailing dark blue lobelia, while the yellow-flowering plants included *Argyranthemum* 'Jamaica Primrose', *Osteospermum* 'Buttermilk', and the golden *Bidens ferulifolia*. We also chose the yellow trailing *Helichrysum petiolatum* 'Aureum' which looked wonderful spilling over the rim of a rich blue pot.

Against the sunny south-facing garage wall we planted a fig (*Ficus* 'Brown Turkey') in an old plastic dustbin buried in the soil – figs fruit far more heavily if their roots are contained. Although we had planted herbs in the vegetable garden, we planted more in the bed with the fig because it is very close to the kitchen so that in winter particularly, picking a sprig of rosemary for the shoulder of lamb would not then involve putting on the wellies.

Directly under the tree, which is a difficult area since it gets little sun in summer, and a lot of wear and tear from the boys, we simply dug out a few centimetres of soil and laid jumbo bark. The wooden edging would ensure that it didn't get kicked everywhere.

A little further away, where there was less danger from feet, we planted a mixture of wild flowers which can tolerate shade in some really poor soil which we had dug out during the excavation of the pond. Nothing much else will thrive in such impoverished soil, but wild flowers actually prefer it. We also replanted some of the shade-tolerant brunnera which has lovely vivid forget-me-not blue flowers and which had been growing there originally, along with some tobacco plants, the night-scented *Nicotiana alata*.

In the main part of the garden we planted a whole range of attractive shrubs and perennials – attractive not only to look at but also to a wide range of wildlife. To draw bees, for example, and ensure pollination in the fruit and vegetable garden, and to lure hoverflies to eat the aphids, we planted thyme, catmint, lavender, asters (*Aster frikartii* 'Mönch') and *Coreopsis verticillata*. For butterflies we planted buddleia (*Buddleia davidii* 'Black Knight'), the iceplant (*Sedum spectabile*) and scabious (*Scabiosa* 'Clive Greaves'). To entice birds into the garden we chose berrying shrubs, including a variety of the native European spindle (*Euonymus europaeus* 'Red Cascade'), the bright red fruits of which attract small birds, particularly robins. It is a striking foliage shrub too, with lovely glowing autumn colour. We also planted the golden cut-leafed elder (*Sambucus racemosa* 'Sutherland Gold'), and evergreen firethorn (*Pyracantha*) which have good berries in the autumn. To cover the fences we chose the large-leafed ornamental vine *Vitis coignetiae* for one side of the garden which has the most beautiful red, crimson and scarlet autumn colour. On the other side, we planted small-flowered *Clematis viticella* – *C.v.* 'Alba Luxurians' which has green-tinged white flowers from July until well into autumn. On the back wall, we planned to put 1m- (3ft)-high squared trellis along the top, which would be planted with the large-leafed Persian ivy (*Hedera colchica* 'Variegata'). This would eventually screen out an ugly electricity pylon in the distance, and also provide a wonderful nesting site for birds.

One of the big pluses in having a long thin garden is that you can divide it up into separate 'rooms' and create a different mood in each one. Our derelict garden, for example, fell naturally into four sections – the patio and pond area, the lawn area surrounded by lots of roses and cottage-style planting, the area that had been the dumping ground and the woodland area at the end. The third section, once it had been cleared and some of the larger shrubs removed, was a decent-sized area about 8 x 6m (25 x 20ft).

Here a secret garden suggested itself which would be completely different in mood, style and colour from the main garden, and with a gazebo tucked in one corner it really would be a place to hide away from the world. Although it might seem rather perverse in the light of the extremely wet early summer of 1997 which followed, we decided to make a dry gravel garden, planted with a range of drought-tolerant plants, which, once established, would cope very well without being watered.

When the ground had been cleared and the perennial weeds killed off with a glyphosate weed-killer, we decided to lay a weed-suppressing membrane over the main area with a thin layer of gravel on top and paving slabs in different shapes and sizes strategically placed throughout as an informal stepping-stone path to the gazebo. Some of the planting would then be done through slits cut in the membrane. This membrane not only keeps the weeds at bay, but also helps conserve moisture in the soil.Unlike black polythene, which does the same job, it allows water through. Gravel laid directly on to the soil doesn't work as well because weeds can grow through it unless you lay it really thickly, and if you do have more than about 2cm (less than 1in) of gravel on the surface, it not only ridges up and doesn't look good, but also becomes difficult to walk on.

The one minor disadvantage of using the membrane is that plants cannot seed themselves as successfully as they can in gravel laid on the soil. Since it was important for the look of this area that some plants, such as bronze fennel and valerian, did seed themselves, we created two curving beds, one in the top right-hand quadrant of the garden, the other in the bottom left, where the membrane was cut away and we planted directly into the soil. The soil was then covered with gravel, so it all looked the same but plants could self-seed successfully into it.

The octagonal gazebo came in kit form and

Above and right: The dry gravel garden is, as planned, quite different in mood to the rest of the garden, with a successful blend of strong architectural shapes like the leaves of the spiky cordyline, clouds of soft silvery foliage and 'hot' flower colours. It was quite a large area, but in just a couple of months, the planting has grown so much that it no longer feels anything like as large.

was relatively easily assembled by two people without much experience of DIY. Since it was sited beneath the purple-leafed plum (*Prunus pissardii*) and the orange-chestnut colour of the treated timber did not really go harmoniously with the foliage, we stained it with an opaque, water-based woodstain. To tone in with the mood and colours of the planting scheme we had selected for the area, we chose a silver-grey shade.

We wanted a focal point in the centre of the gravel garden, something glimpsed through the arch as you looked from the house, which would invite you to explore further up the garden. We also wanted the focal point to catch your eye as you sat in the gazebo looking out at the secret garden, so we took one line straight through the middle of the arch and another from the centre of the front of the gazebo, and where they crossed was the perfect spot for our focal point. For this we chose a simple terracotta Ali-baba pot because of its smooth clean lines. It would have looked good left unplanted, but since we wanted to emphasize the theme of the garden, we planted it with trailing *Lotus berthelotii*, a sun-loving, drought-tolerant, trailing plant with very fine, needle-like, silver leaves and bright scarlet-orange flowers like miniature parrots' beaks.

Another feature in the secret

Silver plants for a dry garden
Artemisia
Senecio (*Brachyglottis greyii*)
Caryopteris x clandonensis
Convolvulus cneorum
Lavender
Curry plant (*Helichrysum italicum*)
Catmint (*Nepeta faassenii*)
Russian sage (*Perovskia*)
Cotton lavender (*Santolina*)
Lambs' ears (*Stachys byzantina*)
Atriplex hamilus
Eleagnus 'Quicksilver'
Hebe pinguifolia 'Pageii'
Coyote willow (*Salix alba sericea*)
Germander (*Teucrium Fruticans*)

garden was a piece of modern sculpture – three slender stainless-steel corkscrews of different heights grouped in a triangle. In fact they are very inexpensive plant supports (the three cost less than £15 altogether), designed for greenhouse tomatoes to climb up, but they looked so striking in their own right that we simply stuck them in the ground and left them unplanted.

Drought-loving plants

Despite the heavy rains of early summer 1997, there is no doubt that the underlying trend in our weather is towards drier summers, and more importantly much drier winters when traditionally the reservoirs have filled up to supply our needs throughout the rest of the year. The result is hosepipe bans in many parts of the country and the realization that we have to think again, long-term, about the plants we can grow successfully.

If that sounds depressing, it really shouldn't, because there are some wonderfully exciting plants that thrive in hot dry conditions, as you'll know if you've had holidays in the Mediterranean, or further afield in South Africa or Mexico – lavenders, thymes, spiky yuccas, cistus, helianthemums, diascias, abutilons and so forth. Also on the plus side is the fact that while many of these slightly tender plants would succumb to frost in wetter conditions, they stand a greater chance of surviving the winter in dry soils, because it's the combination of cold and wet that is most likely to kill them.

HOW TO RECOGNIZE
DROUGHT-TOLERANT PLANTS

If you are planting with drought in mind, it obviously helps to learn a bit about plants before you set off for the garden centre by consulting a good reference book, but there are some simple visual clues as to which plants are most likely to be drought-tolerant.

To start with, almost all grey- and silver-leafed plants will thrive in these conditions, so you will be pretty safe with plants such as lavender, artemisia, lamb's ears (*Stachys byzantina*), brachyglottis (still sometimes called senecio) and *Convolvulus cneorum*. The reason is that the silvery colour, which helps reflect heat away from the leaf, actually comes from a covering of very fine hairs which traps moist air between itself and the leaf's surface. This not only prevents the leaf scorching or shrivelling up, but it also means the plant needs to extract less moisture from the soil via its roots. These hairs become transparent when they're wet –

'Hot' flowers for a dry garden
Cistus purpureus
Crocosmia 'Emberglow'
Eccremocarpus scaber
Eschscholzia californica 'Inferno'
Helianthemum 'Fire Dragon'
Lotus berthelottii
Mesembryanthemum (*Dorotheanthus*)
Osteospermum 'Tresco Purple'
Phygelius 'African Queen'
Portulaca
Pinapple broom (*Cytisus battandieri*)
Spanish broom (*Spartium junceum*)
Asphodeline luteus
Red Hot Poker (Kniphosia 'Bressingham Comet')

that's why silver leaves look much greener after a shower.

Since plants lose moisture through their leaves, drought-lovers never have large fleshy ones. Some have no leaves worthy of the name, like certain brooms and gorse, or have very small leaves, like lavender, cotton lavender (*Santolina chamaecyparissus*) and rue. Others have very narrow leaves, like pinks (*Dianthus*) and the trailing silver *Lotus berthelotii*, or very delicate, lacy, finely divided ones, like the artemisias or *Pyrethrum* 'Silver Feather'. They sometimes have large but very jagged ones, like the globe thistle (*Echinops ritro*) and the sea holly (*Eryngium*), so that they cover the maximum amount of space and absorb as much light as possible without having a large surface area through which to lose moisture.

A number of Mediterranean plants, such as rosemary, lemon verbena (*Lippia citriodora*), lavender, sage and thyme, also have aromatic oils in their leaves which on hot days float like a miasma just above the surface of the leaves and deflect heat. These plants release aromatic oils into the air when the leaves are crushed, or even just brushed against, so plant them at the front of a border or on the corner of a busy thoroughfare, where you are most likely to brush against them. A few, like

Far left: The planting style of the dry gravel garden writ small, with spiky variegated sisyrinchiums growing with 'hot' magenta Osteospermum *'Tresco Purple' and grey brachyglottis.*

Left: To try and combat the terrible weed problem that our garden shares with almost all derelict gardens, we are laying a weed-suppressing membrane over the cleared soil and under the gravel. As it turned out, even this was not strong enough to prevent some bindweed pushing through, but the problem would have been much worse without it.

Above: To allow some of the plants to self-seed through the gravel into the soil beneath, we created two large planting areas without membrane.

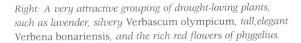

Right: A very attractive grouping of drought-loving plants, such as lavender, silvery Verbascum olympicum, *tall, elegant* Verbena bonariensis, *and the rich red flowers of phygelius.*

thyme, can withstand being trodden on to some degree, so they are ideal for planting in paving where they will spread and form a fragrant carpet.

Mediterranean herbs with narrow leaves, like rosemary and lavender, also protect themselves from heat and drought by the arrangement of their very fine, needle-like leaves. These are arranged in such a way that they shade each other and only a percentage of them is exposed to the sun at any one time. The same is true of desert cacti which have very deep grooves, casting shadows, so that only a small proportion of the plants' surface area is exposed to the sun.

Other drought-loving plants, such as yuccas, some spurges like *Euphorbia myrsinites*, houseleeks (*Sempervivum*), and Livingstone daisies (formerly *Mesembryanthemum* but now renamed *Dorotheanthus*), have thick fleshy leaves in which they can store water and draw on it when they cannot obtain it from the soil. Some, like bergenias and many evergreen shrubs, have leaves which aren't particularly thick but are as tough and leathery as old boots and so are in no danger of shrivelling up. Others still, like the spurges, have a waxy coating to protect their surface and the slight whitish bloom it gives the leaves also helps deflect the heat.

It's true that it is largely by their foliage that you can identify drought-tolerant plants, since all plants must have leaves if they themselves are to survive but need flowers only if they want to reproduce themselves. Drought-tolerant plants often bear spectacular flowers with brightly coloured petals to attract the insects they need for pollination and indeed some of the brightest-coloured flowers, such as mesembryanthemums and gazanias, will close in dull or wet weather because the insects aren't flying, so it's a waste of energy

> 6 *Most drought-tolerant plants thrive on poor soil, and they won't thank you for over-generous feeding* 9

opening. Some of these plants have flowers which are very short-lived, perhaps lasting only a day – like cistus and helianthemums – but they are produced in profusion as the plant tries desperately to reproduce itself. By dead-heading plants like this, and so not allowing them to set seed, you encourage them to go on flowering for a longer period.

GIVING YOUR PLANTS A FLYING START

Even drought-loving plants need *some* water to grow successfully, particularly when they are newly planted and their roots are not yet well enough established to go seeking for water deep in the soil. So soak them thoroughly before you plant. Holding the pot under water with the top of the compost submerged and waiting until all bubbles have stopped rising is the surest way of getting the rootball thoroughly soaked. If you plant in a very dry spell, give them a thorough watering every few days, otherwise they really will struggle to get established. For the long term, on a really poor, thin soil, dig in some bulky organic matter, which will increase its ability to hold water.

The soil in our derelict garden was already very free-draining and stony – ideal for drought-loving plants – so we did not need to improve the drainage, but if yours is a heavier soil, you will need to dig in plenty of gravel – at least a bucketful to the square metre to open it up and make it more free-draining – and add a handful or so to each hole as you plant.

Adding organic matter will boost the fertility of the soil a bit as well. It's worth remembering, though, that most drought-tolerant plants thrive on poor soil, and they won't thank you for over-generous feeding. If they get too many nutrients, the resulting growth tends to be lush, soft and sappy and that makes the plants more vulnerable to pests and also to frost in the winter.

Planting up the dry gravel garden

Given the wide range of plants that would tolerate the conditions in the dry gravel area of our derelict garden, we fixed on a colour scheme that would blend in with the surroundings, particularly with the purple-leafed plum and one large silver-leafed buddleia over by the fence, so we went for mainly purple, bronze and silver foliage. As for flowers, we chose some very soft pastels – blues and yellows – and some very hot colours, which Gerrie particularly loves, such as scarlets, oranges and golds.

FOLIAGE PLANTS

To fill in a large gap at the boundary between existing shrubs we planted *Rosa glauca*. Its foliage is a wonderful blue-grey tinged with mauve, a shade known in gardening terms as 'glaucus' – hence the rose's botanical name. It also has single carmine-pink flowers in June and attractive, bright red hips in winter, but we chose it primarily for its wonderful leaves. The larger form of silvery catmint (*Nepeta* 'Six Hills Giant'), with its haze of soft mauve-blue flowers all

Architectural plants for a dry garden
Angelica (*Angelica archangelica*)
New Zealand cabbage palm (*Cordyline australis*)
Canary Island date palm (*Phoenix canarensus*)
Loquat (*Eriobotrya japonica*)
Sea holly (*Eryngium variifolium*)
Bronze fennel (*Foeniculum vugare 'Purpureum'*)
Honeybush (*Melianthus major*)
New Zealand flax (*Phormium*)
Acanthus spinosus
Cardoon (*Cynara cardunculus*)
Sisyrinchium
Verbascum 'Arctic Summer'
Verbena bonariensis
Yucca
Crambe cordifolia

summer, was ideal for planting behind our focal point since it provided an attractive background for it without competing for attention. In front of the pot in the centre of the garden there is another silver-leafed plant, *Convolvulus cneorum*, with foliage that gleams like mother-of-pearl and tightly twisted, pink buds that unfurl to pure white trumpets. From a distance it creates a soft grey cloud out of which the pot seems to be rising.

Another excellent plant with grey foliage and soft blue flowers is *Caryopteris x clandonensis*. Grown in ordinary borders it is often attacked by slugs, but another advantage of a gravel garden is that the rough surface keeps most slugs and snails at bay. *Oxalis adenophylla* which forms dense neat clumps has pretty pink-mauve flowers in early summer, but its circles of slender, heart-shaped, pale grey-green leaves are worth having for their own sake.

Most people are familiar with *Helichrysum petiolatum*, even if they don't know its name. It's that trailing plant with felted, round, grey leaves that features in many a hanging basket, but it also scrambles very happily along the ground and Helen often uses it to great effect for filling gaps in a newly planted border. As for the purple and bronze foliage, the striking *Cordyline australis* 'Sundance' has leaves

Right: The gazebo provides a perfect place to sit and contemplate the garden, or merely to sit. It comes in kit form, and rather than leave it orangey chestnut brown, which clashed with the purple-leafed plum, we painted it with a silvery grey opaque woodstain.

Below: The view from the gazebo, looking at the pot and the hazy blue and silver planting surrounding it. Most people know Helichrysum petiolatum *(foreground) as a trailing hanging basket plant, but it will scramble along the ground, too, and is excellent for filling space in a newly planted garden.*

Above: The strong, clean lines of the terracotta Ali-baba pot, planted with fern-like silver Lotus berthelotii *and rising out of a cloud of silvery catmint (*Nepeta*) and Russian sage (*Perovskia*) makes an ideal focal point in the centre of the garden.*

striped with bronze and pink, while purple sage (*Salvia officinalis purpurea*), bronze fennel (*Foeniculum vulgare purpureum*) and bronze sedge (the bronze form of *Carex comans*) were chosen for obvious reasons.

FLOWERS FOR 'HOT' COLOUR
Where flowers rather than foliage were the main reason for a particular choice, we went for hot colours: scarlets, magentas, golds, rich purples. To scramble up the silver-grey gazebo, the Chilean glory flower (*Eccremocarpus scaber*) was the ideal choice with its slender, bright red-and-orange trumpet flowers. It can reach almost 5m (16ft) in a season, and in a free-draining soil will come through most winters. It's worth piling some compost, dead bracken or conifer prunings over its roots because, even if the frost does cut

it back to the ground, the roots may well survive to produce new growth in spring.

Phygelius capensis 'Devil's Tears' has slender trumpet flowers of warm red which are bright orange-scarlet and yellow inside. It is a shrub which grows to about 1.2m (4ft) in height and about the same across, and while it is evergreen it may get cut back to the ground in winter by the frost. Again, giving the roots some protection in winter will usually ensure that the plant produces new growth in the spring.

Crocosmias are good plants in this situation, both for the narrow sword-like leaves and the vibrant colour of their flowers. 'Lucifer' is brilliant scarlet, while 'Emberglow' has arching sprays of small burnt-orange flowers from mid- to late summer. There are many good red hot pokers available now, many of them smaller and more delicate than the rather coarse, chunky ones you used to see in cottage gardens. *Kniphofia triangularis* (also known as *galpinii*) grows to about 60cm (2ft) with slender burnt-orange pokers. In a more subtle colour scheme, the pale yellow 'Little Maid' would be a good choice.

As for bright yellows, they don't come much brighter than the tall and stately *Verbascum* 'Arctic Summer'. From a rosette of very large, silver-felted leaves it throws up a flower spike about 1.8m (6ft) tall which is covered in a bright white bloom – hence the 'Arctic' part of its name – before the individual flowers open to the acid yellow. It's a wonderfully dramatic plant, and most welcome in a newly planted area because it provides height very quickly.

Brachyglottis (formerly *Senecio*) *greyii* is another valuable drought-tolerant shrub which combines

> ❦ *Phygelius capensis 'Devil's Tears' may get cut back to the ground in winter by frost, but giving the roots some protection will usually ensure that the plant produces new growth in spring* ❧

grey felted foliage with acid yellow flowers (in this case a mass of small gold daisies) all summer long. As for rich purples, we chose *Osteospermum* 'Tresco Purple' which stands a much better chance of coming through the winter in dry soil than it would where it is wetter. Hebes also do well in these conditions, both the smaller, grey-leafed, white-flowered var eties such as *Hebe pinguifolia* 'Pagei' and the sage-green-leafed *H. albicans,* and the larger varieties with mauve or purple flowers. We chose a new variety, *H.* 'Sapphire', for its rich flower colour. The tall candelabra -like *Verbena bonariensis* (also called *V. patagonica*) has very small flowers, carried in small clusters at the ends of the stiffly branching stems, but they are such an intense mauve-purple colour that they really catch the eye.

BRILLIANT ANNUALS

As for annuals to give some more-or-less instant colour, the Livingstone daisy *Mesembryanthemum/ Dorotheanthus* is ideal, quickly forming mats of fleshy, pale green foliage which are covered in largish daisies in a wide range of colours from magenta through bright red and orange to yellow and white. They really do need a sunny spot as the flowers open only when the sun is shining and seem to flower much more freely in very poor soil. Another annual we planted was the tall, heavily scented tobacco plant *Nicotiana sylvestris* (in fact it is a short-lived tender perennial, so it is best treated as an annual in this country). It can reach 1.5m (5ft) and is best in part-shade since its flowers close in full sun. We planted it in a corner close to the entrance to the secret garden to provide a fragrant welcome.

BOLD STRUCTURAL PLANTS

The shape of the plants was also a factor in our choice. Spiky plants look wonderful grown in gravel and add to the hot exotic feel. Cordylines and phormiums with their large sword-like leaves make a very strong architectural statement either planted in the gravel or grown in a container, while the smaller sisyrinchiums, especially *Sisyrinchium striatum* 'Aunt May' (also known as 'Variegatum') with its pale sage-green-and-cream variegated leaves and soft yellow flowers in early to mid-summer, is another excellent choice.

Of course, grasses work extremely well in gravel gardens too, adding height and movement, since they sway in the slightest breeze. Among those that like dry conditions are the blue grasses like the tall elegant *Helictotrichon sempervirens* and the smaller steel-blue *Festuca glauca* – look for a variety called 'Elijah Blue' which has particularly bright steel-blue leaves. The giant oat grass (*Stipa gigantea*), so named because it produces seed heads up to 2m (6½ft) tall, loves these conditions, as does the finer and smaller *Stipa tenuissima* which produces silky seed heads that look like smoke. Although some of the sedges like Bowles' golden sedge need quite boggy soil, some are happy in dry soil, such as the bronze form of *Carex comans*. Some people dislike it because they think it looks dead, but it is a wonderful rich bronze colour all year, especially when the sun shines through it.

Bronze fennel is a similar colour, but since its leaves are so fine, the impression is more of a bronze haze. If allowed to flower and set seed, this is a plant that will seed itself everywhere for the following year. It's then a question of simply pulling it out where you don't want it.

Planting too many spiky plants together rather lessens their impact, so for visual contrast, combine them with low-growing, more rounded shapes, such as those of oxalis, *Cistus* x *corbariensis*, hebe, purple sage and cotton lavender. The variety *Santolina neapolitana* 'Edward Bowles' has grey-green foliage and pale creamy yellow flowers, very similar in tone to those of the sisyrinchium.

Maintaining the dry gravel garden

Once the dry gravel garden was planted, all it needed was initial watering in periods of drought to help all the plants get established. (The following year, it would be left to fend for itself.) The garden also needed weeding. In any derelict garden, weeds will inevitably be a problem for the first few years and ours was no exception. In the beds without any planting membrane, bindweed continued to flourish and even where the membrane was laid, in places it pushed its way through. It must be said, though, that the problem would have been infinitely worse without the membrane. Treat it with glyphosate in spring and summer when it is growing strongly – relatively easy to do since it is surrounded by gravel. You'll be lucky to kill it off with just one treatment, but two or three should do the trick. Why 'weedy' means weak and feeble I will never know! Annual weeds that seed in the gravel can be easily dealt with – just pull them out as they appear. If you get into the habit of looking out for weeds every time you go into the garden, and dealing with them on the spot, they are much easier to deal with than if you leave them for a major weeding session every few weeks.

> ❛ Spiky plants look wonderful grown in gravel and add to the hot exotic feel ❜

Above: Our wildlife pond just three months after we dug it out and planted it. All the plants are growing well, and the fact that the water is crystal clear is a sure sign that everything is in a healthy balance.

Left: The mini-bog garden, created in an old brick-built tank, is thriving, with the huge-leafed Gunnera manicata *and one of the irises salvaged from the derelict pond.*

PONDS AND POOLS

There is no doubt that having water in the garden is a real asset. It attracts wildlife to the garden – you will be astonished at how quickly after you have filled a pond with water that the first dragonflies or damselflies are skimming over the surface – and it is an interesting reflective surface mirroring the sky. Of course, if it is moving water, it also adds sound to the garden, a refreshing gentle splashing or trickling which creates a sense of coolness on a hot day, and diverts the ear from the less welcome sounds around you.

Water features in the derelict garden

Right in the middle of the patio of our derelict garden was a circular pond, about 1.8m (6ft) in diameter, with a curved raised lip around it; it was made of cement, but nicely weathered with lots of lichen growing on it. The pool itself, apart from a few very healthy-looking irises growing in it and a few small new water-lily leaves, was a complete mess. There was a crack right round the top of the pond, through which water obviously leaked away, and below it the middle was filled with a

Right: The new water feature on the patio, with the child-safe bubble fountain, bought as a kit, and the Japanese-style planting is the ideal solution to the problem of the derelict pond.

brownish sludge which, on closer inspection, was alive with hundreds of wriggling tadpoles.

It had once been an attractive feature, and rather than fill it in we decided to restore it. One day it would be a water-lily pool once more, but since Gerrie and Neill have a baby son it would be too risky to have standing water until he was older, so in the short term it would become a water feature of a different, safer kind.

The first job was to clear it out and see exactly what lay beneath. In an ideal world we would have waited until all the tadpoles had grown into frogs, but we had to get on, so the next best thing was to empty the pool as carefully as possible and find them a new home. Because frogs will return to breed in the pond where they were spawned two or three years earlier, Gerrie and Neill will have to expect puzzled frogs on the patio for a year or two, but as the next-door neighbour has a pond, they won't have too far to travel to find a substitute.

The irises were certainly worth saving, so we put them into a washing-up bowl with as much wet sludge around the roots as possible and kept them there until we decided what to do with them. If you are renovating a bigger pond and have a number of plants you wish to keep, as well as goldfish, a child's inflatable or collapsible paddling pool makes a very good holding bay. The easiest way to catch any fish is with one of those small fishing nets that bring back memories of rock pools on childhood holidays.

You may find that the plants in your pond are growing in special plastic baskets, in which case it is very simple just to lift them out. If they are growing in the mud at the bottom of the pool, remove them carefully with as much soil as you can. Where possible, use water from the pond so that plants, and any wildlife, do not have to cope with the shock of fresh tap water with all its chemicals as well as the move. As for the remaining water in the pond, scoop it out with a bucket, though if it is very shallow a plastic dustpan does the job more efficiently. While the water can be poured either on to the garden –

waste not, want not! – or down the drain, any sludge should be disposed of on the compost heap if you have one, or on a spare patch of soil, because it could clog the drains.

Once all the sludge, tadpoles, a few mature frogs and the plants had been removed and rehoused or disposed of, we were left with a shallow bowl-shaped pond with a rusty metal fountainhead in the centre and, in the bottom, a series of beds of different depths created out of concrete walls to hold aquatic plants with differing needs. The first job with any newly emptied pond is to scrub it out with a stiff brush to remove the green algae clinging to the bottom. An eggcupful of household bleach added to the water makes the job a little easier.

The bottom was in good shape with no cracks it in, so the next job, perversely, was to make a hole in it – a hole with a plug (obtainable from builders' merchants). With any concrete pool, a drain in the bottom is very useful when you are clearing it out and need to get rid of those last few centimetres of water which are very awkward to siphon or scoop out.

In our pond, in the short term, for reasons that will become clear, the plug would be left out.

Repairing a concrete pond

The best way to mend cracks in any concrete pond is with a specially formulated compound reinforced with glass fibre for repairing ponds, available from any good garden centre with a water-gardening section.

1 Before you start, brush over the area around each crack with a wire brush to remove any debris and to create a rough surface to which the compound will adhere more effectively.

2 Wet the area thoroughly, using a large paint brush or a small hand sprayer, making sure that the inside of the crack is thoroughly moist as well.

3 Mix up the compound and apply it with an old trowel, smoothing it as you go. If the crack or hole is particularly deep, apply a little at a time and let it dry out between applications.

4 When the compound is completely dry, paint it first with a special pond primer and, once that is dry, with pond sealant, a liquid plastic which forms a lasting membrane to ensure that the pool is 100 per cent watertight. It comes in three colours: swimming-pool turquoise, a natural stone colour and black. It is a question of taste, but my choice would be black because you can't then see the bottom, which means you get the sharpest reflections, the depth of the pool appears infinite and it hides any imperfections in the surface better than lighter colours would do. To get the best possible seal, apply one coat vertically and then a couple of days later, when that is completely dry, apply the second coat horizontally – or the other way round.

5 Fill the pool with water and, if it's from the tap, wait at least ten days for all the chemicals, such as chlorine, to evaporate before you put the plants and fish back in.

USING A FLEXIBLE POND LINER

Another way to solve the problem of a leaking concrete pool is to use a flexible pond liner (see pages 52–3), but this works best on a square or rectangular pool and simply would not have worked with our circular pool because there would have been just too much liner to try to lose in neat folds and the concave cement lip meant that there was no way of fixing the liner invisibly at the top.

Converting a pond into a water feature

Once the cracks in our pool had been mended, they were painted with the clear pond primer. Since it wasn't going to function as a pool just yet for safety reasons, and would be filled with soil, it made sense not to paint the inside with black pond sealant at this stage. That could wait until it was ready to resume life as a pond.

Instead, we were ready to convert it into an equally attractive water feature. In the centre was a pebble pool, with a small jet pumping water up and over a circle of pebbles and back into the hidden reservoir underneath them. That way you have the sound and sensation of water but with no danger to small children because there is no standing water.

It is very simply achieved with a kit available from most garden centres, consisting of a black plastic moulded sump to hold the water and a small electric pump, and a lid to fit over it, on to which you then pile pebbles or any other decorative finish – glass beads or coloured crushed glass, perhaps, or even rubber balls in bright colours.

Having filled the bottom of the pond with a deep layer of rubble, and topped it with a thin layer of sand, we put in a slab on which the sump of the bubble fountain would sit. We then packed sand in around it to hold it steady, followed by 15–20cm of ordinary soil for the bog garden. The pump which drives the fountain was connected to a special waterproof outdoor socket, fitted with a circuit breaker for safety, via a duct put in under the patio when it was being relaid – always a good idea to think ahead! Unless you are using a low-voltage DIY system, always get a qualified electrician to handle any installations in the garden.

The final step was to fill the sump with water, put on the black plastic lid, and cover it partly with pebbles and, once the plants were in, partly with the same gravel used to mulch the bog garden.

Most bog gardens are natural in style and usually on the margins of an informal pond, but there is absolutely no reason why you can't have a formal one and indeed bog plants look very good in that setting. But wherever you put it, a bog garden must have some drainage or the soil will become sour and smelly, and the plants won't thrive. And of course that's why we left the plug out of the drainage hole at the bottom of the pond. In the unlikely event of torrential rain, with no escape for the water, the bog garden might even overflow.

2 *It's important that the slab on which the bubble fountain stands is absolutely level. It is sitting on a deep layer of rubble with a layer of sand on top of that.*

3 *With the sump of the bubble fountain in position, pack sand under the rim to hold it steady.*

4 *A layer of topsoil mixed with peat and grit about 15-20 centimetres deep goes on top of the sand for planting.*

1 *We made a large drainage hole in the bottom of the pond – essential for the health of the plants while it functions as a bog garden. When it eventually becomes a pond again, it can be sealed with a plug.*

We put the irises back in, along with marsh marigolds, *Houttuynia cordata* 'Chameleon' with bright variegated gold, red and green leaves, some sweet flags (*Acorus*) and the dwarf bulrush (*Typha minima*). The very rampant plants such as the bulrushes were grown in special plastic baskets to restrict their ambitions, while others like the houttuynia, not quite so rampant, were planted directly into the soil and allowed a bit of elbow room. The soil was then covered with the same colours as the larger ones in the centre, which will not only help conserve moisture in the soil, but will also add the formal look.

5 *To make it easier to remove the plants later, and control the more ambitious ones, plant in special aquatic plastic mesh baskets.*

6 *After you have put the pump inside the sump, filled it with water and put the lid on, hide the black plastic with a layer of attractive pebbles.*

Mini-bog garden

An old brick-built tank next to the garage in the derelict garden seemed to Helen to be an ideal site for another little bog garden. It was about 1m

7 *The small bubble jet is enough to wet the pebbles and bring out their lovely colours, and to give you the gentle sound of moving water.*

(3ft) deep and about 1.2m (4ft) long and 60cm (2ft) wide and its function, apart from supporting a galvanized water tank, now rusted through, was unclear. The bottom was cracked, but this time, since it did not need to be watertight at any stage and some drainage was essential, there was no point in repairing it. Instead we half-filled it with rubble, laid as evenly as possible, followed this with a layer of sand to level out the surface and then lined it with a butyl-rubber pond liner with a few drainage slits cut in the bottom. Having filled it to within 15cm (6in) of the top with garden soil mixed with compost (fine to use some compost in a bog garden but not for pond plants in baskets; see page 56) we then topped it up with water and trimmed the edges of the liner neatly.

We decided to go for a spectacular plant as the centrepiece – giant rhubarb (*Gunnera manicata*), which produces leaves up to 1m (3ft) long. We planted one of the irises from the pond and some creeping jenny around the edge to soften the out-line, and then covered the surface with gravel.

People with small gardens are often frightened of enormous plants, but they can add an element of drama to a small area, and can also, ironically, make the garden appear larger. In three months the gunnera had grown to about 2½ m (about 8 ft).

The pond in the organic garden

In our organic garden a wildlife pond was a must. Not only does it attract a whole range of attractive creatures to the garden – there are few colours more dazzling in nature than the electric blue of dragonflies and damselflies – but it also attracts those which will eat many of the pests, like toads and frogs, hedgehogs, and birds that come to drink and stay to feed on flying insects as well as on slugs and snails.

Given its vital role in pest control, the ideal site for the wildlife pond was as close to the fruit and vegetable garden as possible. Space was at a premium, so we decided to make a slender oval pond about 2m x 80cm (6ft 6in by 2ft 8in) at the junction of the south-facing bed and the new bed in front of the espaliered fruit screen.

In an ideal world, a wildlife pond should be a bit bigger than ours, but it was large enough. What you must not compromise on, though, is the depth. It *must* be at the very least 60cm (2ft) deep in parts to give wildlife a chance to escape from herons and cats and from ice if the pond freezes over in winter. Incidentally, one useful tip to protect fish from herons is to place a length of black plastic drainpipe along the bottom of the pond. The fish can dart into it when the heron appears and even its long neck and beak cannot get hold of them then.

Making a wildlife pond

You can buy pre-formed ponds from the garden centre, and while many of them are now avail-able in black rather than the unnatural turquoise they used to come in, most of the shapes are very artificial, like pieces of root ginger, and they're not all that easy to install. Have you ever tried digging a hole the shape of a piece of root ginger? It's better to create a simple informal shape of your own – a rough oval, say – and use a butyl-rubber or plastic liner. To work out the size you need, add twice the maximum depth to the length and twice the maximum depth to the width and add 60cm (2ft) overlap to each. So if the pond is 3m (10ft) long, 2m (6½ft) wide and 75cm (2½ft) deep, you need a liner at least 5.1m (17ft) long and 4.1m (13½ft) wide.

DIGGING OUT THE POND
1 Mark out the shape of the pond with hosepipe or washing line and dig it out to a depth of about 10cm (4in).
2 Hammer in a series of pegs around the edge, levelling each one against the one before with a spirit level. The top of any pond must be level.

Water always lies level, and if your pond isn't, you'll see exposed pond liner at the high end which will destroy any illusion of it being a natural pond. Before you start, make life simple for yourself by marking each peg with a line 5cm (2in) from the top; then, when you've hammered them all in, level the soil to the marks.

3 Start digging about 15cm (6in) inside the pegs, saving the topsoil in one pile to be used elsewhere in the garden and the subsoil, which is useless for growing most plants, in another. Once the pond is dug, incidentally, you get a rare opportunity to see the structure of your soil very clearly – the thinnish layer of topsoil, then a broader band of subsoil, which is almost always lighter in colour, and then the substrate.

4 As you dig, be sure to leave a broad shelf about 20cm (8in) down over at least half the perimeter, on which to grow marginal plants – those that like their feet in shallow water. Be sure, too, to create one gently sloping area so that any creatures that chance to fall in, such as hedgehogs, can make their way out again, although the shelf can help here too.

If you want the pond surrounded by grass or planting rather than stone slabs, which never look very natural, you need to hide the liner under the soil, so dig a trench all the way round the outside about 15cm (6 in) deep.

LINING THE POND

1 To prevent stones and roots in the soil from puncturing the liner you need first to lay an underliner – we used a special one, but you can use old carpet (the *only* place old carpet would

❛ People with small gardens are often frightened of enormous plants, but they can add an element of drama to a small area, and can, ironically, make the garden appear larger ❜

be allowed in this garden!) or blankets, if you have any. Smooth the underliner out as best you can, then push it with a broom into the bottom of the pond, the back of the shelf and down into the trench around the top, folding the excess into neat creases. Alternatively, if you have a large pond with very gently sloping sides, line the pond with 3cm (1–1½in) or so of sand. If it has steepish sides, as ours did, though, all the sand would simply fall to the bottom.

2 Spread the liner on top – definitely a two-person job – and push it carefully down to the bottom of the pond with the broom, taking great care not to disturb the underliner. Don't worry too much about smoothing out all the creases at this stage – the weight of the water will do that for you to a large extent.

3 Fill the pond with the hose running gently, which will take longer than you think.

4 When the water is within a few centimetres of the top, turn off the hose and then start smoothing out the liner around the top. Push it down into the trench round the outside, fill the trench in with soil to hold the liner in place and trim it at the top of the furthest edge.

5 If you plan to plant around the pond, place upside-down turves round the edge of the pond, coming slightly over the edge so that the liner is completely hidden from view. Turf is very useful here because the roots of the grass hold the soil together and prevent it all slipping into the water. However, if some soil does fall into the water, it doesn't matter, because there will be soil in the pond anyway and it helps clear the water. Where the pond is to be surrounded by lawn, cover the filled-in trench with turf – the right way up this time.

Left: The wildlife pond blends in so well with its surroundings it's hard to believe it was only made a few months earlier.

Below: The cheerful yellow flowers of the marsh marigold (Caltha palustris), a marginal aquatic plant, growing in a basket on the specially created ledge around the edge of the pool.

1 *Use a hose to mark out the shape of your pool. Free-flowing curves look more natural.*

2 *A broom is the ideal tool to push the underliner into all the crevices.*

4 *Surplus turf, used upside down, is ideal for covering the edge of the liner where the pond joins a bed or border.*

5 *Where the pool joins the lawn, though, use turf the right way up to edge it and conceal the liner.*

3 *Broom, bodies and bricks are all useful in getting the butyl liner into position.*

6 *Don't worry if the pond looks like pea soup immediately after planting. It will soon clear.*

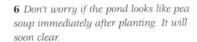

STOCKING THE POND

If you have filled the pond with tap water, wait for at least a week or even ten days before you put in the plants. Tap water contains chlorine which plants and pond life dislike, but it will evaporate in a week or so. After planting, leave the plants to settle for a couple of weeks before you put in any wildlife. If possible, add a bucket of water from someone else's pond. That will contain the microscopic creatures which will help your pond achieve the natural balance you want. You need to decide whether or not to add fish. Goldfish eat tadpoles and other pond creatures, so it is usually a case of one or the other, and if you are aiming to create a real wildlife pond, perhaps you should give the goldfish a miss.

PLANTING THE POND

When it comes to choosing plants for your pond, you need three different kinds – the deep-water plants, such as water lilies, marginals, such as rushes, irises and kingcups; and oxygenating plants, such as Canadian pondweed (*Elodea crispa*), which are more functional than decorative since they keep the water healthy and provide oxygen for both plants and wildlife.

If you want to plant straight into the pool, you'll need to spread a layer of soil 8cm (3in or so) over the liner before you

---

Pond plants

Marginals (growing in water up to 23cm (9in) deep):

weet flag
(*Acorus calamus* 'Variegatus')

Marsh marigold
(*Caltha palustris*)

Houttuynia cordata
'Chameleon'

Corkscrew rush
(*Juncus effusus* Spiralis)

Water forget-me-not
(*Myosotis scorpioïdes*
'Mermaid')

Lobelia cardinalis

Zebra rush
(*Schoenoplectus*
tabernaemontani 'Zebrinus')

Dwarf bulrush
(*Typha minima*)

Pickeral weed
(*Pontederia cordata*)

Deep water plants:

Water hawthorn
(*Aponogeton distachyos*)

Water lily
(*Nymphaea odorata minor* or
N. pygmaea)

---

fill it with water. Since liners can be punctured by stones every bit as easily from above as from below, sieve the soil carefully first. Once you add the water the pond will look very muddy for a day or two, but the soil will settle eventually and the water will clear. Then you can plant straight into the bottom.

Our pond was too steep-sided for that, so we planted everything, except the oxygenators, in special plastic-mesh baskets. We chose curved baskets, which sit on the curving shelf perfectly. The baskets control the ambitions of over-vigorous pond plants and of course make it very easy to remove the plants for dividing up once they get too big. Fine-mesh baskets don't need lining, but if they are the coarser type, line them with sacking to keep the soil in. Fill the baskets with ordinary garden soil. You can buy special aquatic soil, but whatever you do, don't use ordinary potting compost. It is rich in nutrients which will encourage algae to grow like mad and turn your pond into pea soup.

Once the baskets are planted up, add a layer of gravel to help keep the soil in place and prevent it floating off into the water. If you have fish it will also prevent them nosing around in the mud and disturbing your plants.

As for deciding which marginals to grow, you really are spoilt for choice. Certainly you should bear in mind contrasting shapes and habits, so be sure to include some tall spiky plants such as the variegated sweet rush (*Acorus gramineus* 'Variegatus'), an iris such as *Iris pseudacorus*, the miniature bulrush (*Typha minima*) and *Schoenoplectus tabernaemontani* 'Zebrinus'. You'll also want some tall bushy plants such as the spectacular *Lobelia cardinalis* with beetroot-coloured leaves and vivid scarlet flowers; some smaller bushy ones, like the golden marsh marigold (*Caltha palustris*) and the brightly variegated *Houttuynia cordata* 'Chameleon'; and some plants whose growth floats on the water like the blue-flowered water forget-me-not (*Myosotis scorpioïdes* 'Mermaid').

❛ *Be sure to choose a water lily that is the right size for your pond* ❜

Water lilies are a must but some are very large indeed, so be sure you choose one that is the right size for your pond. In a very small pond, look for *Nymphaea pygmaea*, *N. x helvola* or *N. odorata*, which come in white, yellow or pink.

There are two schools of thought when it comes to planting deep-water plants like water lilies. Conventional wisdom suggests that you put them on a stack of bricks or old pots so that they are just under the water, and remove one brick at a time as the leaves reach the surface until the basket is finally resting on the bottom. Other people just put them straight on to the bottom and let the leaves make their way to the surface from there. If you don't want to get your arm wet, slide two lengths of rope or strong string through holes in the basket, grasp them at one end and, with another person standing on the other side of the pond holding the other ends, lower it into position and then pull out the strings.

As for oxygenating plants, you'll need two bundles for every square metre of surface area. You can either plant them in a basket of their own and set that on the bottom of the pond or, if there are a few centimetres of soil on the bottom, toss the bundles in and the lead weights which tie the shoots together will take them down where they will root. Alternatively use a floating oxygenator such as *Ceratophyllum demersum*, which looks rather like mare's tail and in summer floats just below the surface of the water.

Once the pool is planted up, it will take a few weeks to settle down and may look a bit pea-soupy again in the meantime. If the algae which cause the greenness don't clear after a few weeks, or you find blanketweed, a form of algae which forms a slimy green mass on the surface of the pond, you could add mats made from barley straw which seem to be very effective in combating the problem. Weight them down with string and a stone so that they are not floating on the surface.

Another way of controlling blanketweed is to put a stick into the middle and wind it round and round, wrapping the weed on to it. If you do this, leave the blanketweed close to the edge of the pond for a day or two to allow any pond creatures caught in it to escape back into the water.

WINTER PRECAUTIONS

In very cold winter weather, float a rubber ball on the surface of the pond. If it freezes over, the ball will absorb the expansion of the water as it turns to ice. If the top of the pond stays frozen for some days, make a hole in the ice to allow the escape of noxious gases that build up under the ice. Do not under any circumstances smash the ice, since the shock waves could kill the fish. Instead place a pan of boiling water on the surface to melt a circular hole. It is extremely unlikely in this country that a pond of 60m (2ft) deep will freeze solid, so the fish and other pond creatures should come through unscathed

VEGETABLES

One of the very real and tangible benefits of learning to garden organically is that you grow highly nutritious fruit and vegetables, free from all the chemicals used to produce them commercially. In an average-sized garden you can create a productive area large enough to make a significant – and delicious – contribution to your diet, even if you can't be wholly self-sufficient.

We decided to allocate about one third of our organic garden to fruit and vegetables – the area at the far end which included the concrete hard standing and the green metal shed, as well as part of the lawn.

When we had removed the shed and taken up the concrete, the next stage was to strip off the turf. In an ideal world we would have covered the grass with black polythene or old carpet for a year to exclude all light so that the grass would die off and rot down into the soil as valuable organic matter. We could not wait a year, though, so we stripped off the turf, and stacked it in a pile to use elsewhere in the garden – around the edge of the pond, for example, to hide the top of the black liner and at the bottom of planting holes since it helps conserve moisture and, as it breaks down, provides valuable organic matter for the plants, and finally as a loam pile (see page 84).

Above: Luscious lettuce leaves with not a pest or disease in sight.

Making raised beds

The best way to grow vegetables is in a bed system, with raised beds about 1.2m (4ft) wide. This means that you can both put water and nutrients, such as compost, precisely where they are needed – on the cropping area – and, most important, that you can easily work from the paths on each side without needing to tread on the beds and so damage the structure of the soil.

Above and right: One of the real benefits of growing vegetables is how quickly you are rewarded for your labours. Three months after we built our four vegetable beds, they had been cropping well for a few weeks with plenty more to come.

Right: It's easier to complete the sides of the raised beds before you hammer the pegs into the ground.

The length of the beds is less important, dependent more on how much space you have available and how you want to lay them out, although do bear in mind that if they are too long, it's human nature to be tempted to walk across the bed rather than round it.

We had room for four beds in our plot, each 3m (10ft) long with paths 60cm (2ft) wide between them to allow easy access with a wheelbarrow. With a greater number of beds, the centre path would still need to be 60cm (2ft) wide to cope with a wheelbarrow, but the paths between the beds on either side would need to be only 40cm (16in) since you just need room to walk between them. The simplest way to make paths which are clean underfoot but keep weeds at bay is to lay a heavy-duty woven membrane and scatter coarse bark chippings or even gravel on top of it.

Raised beds have the added advantage, particularly on heavy clay soils, of helping improve the drainage. Simply adding organic matter to the soil year after year will mound the beds, so it makes sense to contain them with wooden boards. Old floorboards will do the job if you can find them. If not, use new timber (see page 32), cut to the lengths you need by the timber merchant. Untreated timber will last only five to ten years, but can easily be replaced when it does start to rot.

1 Measure out the beds using pegs at each corner and string tied tautly between them. A very simple way to check that the corners are exact right angles is to make a mark along one side of the string 3cm *or* 3in from the corner, then make another mark 4cm *or* 4in along the other string from the same peg, then measure across the corner between the two marks and the distance should be 5cm *or* 5in: Pythagoras's theorem in

> *Raised beds have the advantage of helping improve drainage*

action! If the answer is not 5cm *or* 5in, adjust the strings until it is. Check all the corners in the same way.

2 The easiest way to make the edging is to nail two 2 x 2in pegs 30cm (1ft) long, sharpened at one end, at either end of one of the long planks, plus similar pegs evenly spaced at about 1m (3ft) apart along its length. (While you buy timber in metric lengths, the sizes are still given in inches, presumably because it is much easier to say 'two by two' than '5.1 x 5.1 cm'.) The top of each peg should be about one third of the way down the plank. Placing the wooden pegs carefully into the corners you have marked out with string, hammer them into the soil, until the bottom of the plank is just above soil level. It's best to hammer each end down just a little at a time to make sure that the pegs go in straight.

3 Do the other long side in the same way, then nail the two short planks on to the pegs.

Crop rotation

Our four beds were going to be used for four different types of crop, all from the same family or all having very similar needs, so they would need slightly different preparation. It matters which crop is grown in which bed because, for the healthiest crops and best use of the nutrients in the soil, you need to practise crop rotation. That means growing different crops in each bed every year, following each other in a particular order to make maximum use of all the nutrients in the soil. Crop rotation also means that, since different vegetable families are prone to different diseases, there is far less chance of disease building up in the soil.

Brassicas (the cabbage family) always follow

the legumes (peas and beans) because the latter leave valuable nitrogen in the soil from which the brassicas can benefit. The legumes move into the potato bed while the potatoes move into the root vegetable bed (carrots, parsnips, kohl rabi and so on) and the roots move into the bed the brassicas occupied the previous year. Over four years each crop is grown in a different bed each year. Other crops that are very quick-maturing, such as salads of different kinds, are grown as 'catch' crops in beds alongside slower-growing crops. While crops like lettuce tend to be largely free of diseases, it is still better to avoid growing them in the same soil season after season.

Another way of preventing pests and diseases from becoming established is to keep the vegetable garden tidy by removing dead and dying foliage regularly. Most spent crops – the foliage of peas and beans, for instance – can go on the compost heap.

Obviously the choice of crops you can grow is huge and only a small selection can be covered in this book. As space in most gardens is limited it's important to make the best use of it by growing organically those vegetables that you really enjoy eating and that are expensive to buy in the shops.

THE POTATO BED

The first bed was the potato bed, in which we were also going to grow tomatoes (they belong to the same family) and courgettes (members of a different family but, like the other two, very greedy feeders). To feed their prodigious appetites, this bed needed both manure and compost. Always buy well-rotted manure – try the local riding stables or a friendly farmer – which is bulky but without too much visible straw. As it rots down, straw robs the soil of nitrogen, which rather defeats the object of the exercise. As for compost, it's unlikely that you will inherit a large pile of the

Keep the vegetable garden tidy by removing dead foliage regularly

stuff as Jani and Rob did, and yours won't be ready yet, but you can buy organic compost quite easily now from garden centres. Look for the Soil Association's mark on the bag: that is your guarantee that it really is organic.

Perhaps one of the most striking things about gardening organically is how little organic matter you need. Manure, for instance, is applied at the rate of just one spadeful to a square metre, while compost is applied at the rate of two spadesful to the same area. Traditional vegetable growers like to apply manure in the autumn, but organic growers don't, on the grounds that many of the nutrients simply leach away during the winter, add to the problem of nitrates in the water table and go to waste. So apply it in spring, just before you are going to plant, and fork it lightly into the surface, to about a spade's depth, disturbing the soil as little as possible. Vegetables are annual crops, so you don't need to cultivate the soil too deeply.

The key to growing potatoes successfully is to exclude all light and prevent the potatoes turning green, which makes them inedible. The traditional way is to earth them up – pile soil up on top of them once the first shoots appear, and keep adding more earth as they grow until the potato patch looks like a heavily ploughed field with deep ridges and furrows. However, rather than earthing them up, grow them flat, under a mulch – a layer of biodegradable paper (available from good garden centres or by mail order), with grass cuttings piled on top. Lay the paper over the soil and weight it down with soil at the edges. Then make cross-shaped cuts in the paper in rows 20cm (8in) from the end plank and about 35cm (14in) apart. Fold back the corners of each cross, to allow you to get a trowel in and excavate a hole about 15cm (6in) deep. As an easy guide, the blade of a trowel is about 15cm (6in) long.

Above: The potatoes, mulched with lawn clippings on top of the horticultural paper and kept well watered, are doing very well.

Left: If possible grow organic seed potatoes which have already been chilted (sprouted). Plant them with most of the sprouts at the top.

Top left: Grow potatoes through a special horticultural paper mulch to exclude light. You need to dig a hole about the depth of the trowel.

Right: Red, spring and ordinary – a variety of different onions.

Below: Delicious new potatoes harvested less than three months after planting.

In a very small space it is not worth growing maincrop potatoes, so instead grow earlies – new potatoes – or salad varieties such as 'Charlotte' and 'Pink Fir Apple' which are expensive to buy.

Use pre-chitted potatoes – special seed potatoes bought from the garden centre or by mail order and not what you might find lurking at the back of the vegetable rack in the kitchen – with small healthy shoots coming from the eyes. Look for organically grown seed potatoes or at least those that haven't been treated with chemicals after harvesting. If you are lucky, your garden centre may have them. If not, you can get them mail order from specialist organic gardening companies.

Place the potato in the bottom of the hole, with most of the shoots pointing upwards. Then fill in with soil and unfold the corners of the paper mulch so that almost all the soil is covered. Once you have planted all the potatoes, spread a thick layer of grass clippings over the top and wait for the first shoots to appear. It's worth checking from time to time that all the shoots are growing up through the slits in the paper, and not growing along the soil underneath it. If you do find any, ease them out through the nearest slit. As the shoots grow, keep adding grass clippings. Once the potatoes are in flower, they need copious amounts of water to ensure the biggest possible crop. Planted around Easter, they should be ready for harvesting in June or July.

Good varieties 'Pentland Javelin', 'Charlotte', 'Pink Fir Apple'.

Tomatoes

Members of the same family as potatoes and hence grown in the same bed, tomatoes cannot be planted outside until all danger of frost is past, so either start them from seed indoors in late spring or buy plants from the garden centre. Buy organically produced seed if possible. Again, if your local garden centre doesn't stock it, you should be able to get it mail order from specialist organic suppliers. If you can't, make sure that you buy seed which has not been treated with chemicals after harvesting.

Plant the young tomato plants about 50cm (20in) apart and stake each one with a 1.2m (4ft) cane. Using soft string, tie the stem to the cane every 15–20 cm (6–8in) as it grows. A mulch of comfrey leaves spread on the soil will boost fertility. Once the plant has produced four trusses or clusters of tiny fruits (three in colder gardens), pinch out the top of each plant and keep pinching out the side shoots that appear in the angle between the leaves and the main stem so that all the plant's energy goes to produce more fruits. Pick the tomatoes as soon as they are ripe to encourage the plant to go on producing more.

Good varieties 'Gardeners' Delight', 'Rouge de Mamande' (beefsteak type), 'Tumbler' (bush type).

Easy vegetables

Carrots
'Early Nantes' or
'Autumn King'

Courgettes
'Burpee Golden Zucchini'

New or salad potatoes
'Charlotte' or
'Pentland Javelin'

Onion sets
'Jet Set' or 'Red Supreme'

Peas
'Early onward' or
'Sugar Snap'

Radish
'French Breakfast'

Runner beans
'Painted Lady' or
'Polestar'

Lettuce
'Lollo Rosso' or 'Salad Bowl'

Spring onions
'White Lisbon'

Cabbage
'Minicole' or 'January King'

Broccoli
'Green Comet' or 'Jewel'

Tomatoes
'Gardeners' Delight' or
'Tumbler'

Courgettes

Courgettes enjoy the same conditions as potatoes – good rich soil and plenty of moisture. They are rewarding to grow from seed because the seeds are so large that even the first pair of leaves is a very satisfying size. Start them off on the windowsill in late April and plant them out at the end of May/beginning of June when all danger of frost is past. I say 'them', but for a small plot one plant will probably provide enough courgettes. Like tomatoes, they will benefit from a mulch of comfrey leaves. Pick the courgettes when they are small. If you leave them to turn into marrows, they are not so good to eat and the plant will stop producing more.

Good varieties 'Defender', 'Burpee Golden Zucchini'.

THE ROOT CROP BED

Once crop rotation is established the root crop bed will not need any compost added because there will be enough nutrients left in the soil from the brassicas the previous year. If you have any leaf mould, add that because it is an excellent soil conditioner but is low in nutrients. In the first year, though, you will need to add compost – two spadesful to the square metre – and fork it in lightly.

Carrots

Carrots are a great crop to grow organically because, freshly pulled, they taste absolutely delicious. Grown organically, and so free of all chemicals, they can be eaten in their entirety, skin and all, and of course the skin is the most nutritious part.

The main rules for sowing carrot seed are designed to defeat the carrot fly, which is the major pest of this crop. Since carrot fly is most active in late spring, sowing after the beginning of June is a good idea. If you have to sow before then, make sure that you sow as thinly as possible – a seed or two every 4cm (1½in) is ideal – so that you won't have to thin the carrots when they have germinated. It's the smell of the carrots, released when the soil is disturbed by thinning, that attracts the fly. Sow in rows about 25cm (10in) apart and in succession, leaving a week or so between to ensure continuity of cropping.

To ward off carrot fly, a physical barrier is by far the most effective way. Some gardeners erect a screen of garden fleece 60cm (2ft) high because the flies don't fly any higher than that, but to prevent the occasional gust of wind blowing them over, a tunnel consisting of fleece stretched over a series of hoops and tucked firmly into the soil at both ends is safer.

At first, you may need to weed between rows. Do it in the evening if at all possible, because any disturbance of the soil could release the carrot smell which attracts carrot fly, and it is less active in the evening. Water regularly and evenly if the weather is dry. Don't let the carrots dry out and then give them a drenching as that will cause the carrots to split. They should be ready by mid- to late summer. The longer you leave them in the ground, the bigger they get, and the less good the flavour.

Good varieties Earlies: 'Early Nantes'; maincrop: 'Autumn King', 'New Red Intermediate'; short varieties (good on stony soils where the long varieties split and twist): 'Favourite', 'Nelson'.

> ❛ *To ward off carrot fly, a physical barrier is the most effective way* ❜

Parsnips
Parsnips are best started off in modules (see page 69) and planted out later.
Good varieties 'Arrow', 'White Gem'.

Kohl rabi
A good quick-maturing root vegetable, this has a turnip-like flavour and can be eaten cooked or grated raw in salads. Best started off in modules.
Good varieties 'Green Vienna', 'Purple Vienna'.

THE BRASSICA BED
Add compost at the usual rate to the brassica bed and fork it lightly in. You can grow different types of cabbage – spring, summer and autumn/ winter – to give you a crop all through the year. They are best planted as small plants, either grown from seed in a special seed bed to allow for easy thinning out and transplanting or in modules (see page 69), or bought from the garden centre. For autumn/winter cabbage, sow in spring and plant out in midsummer 45cm (18in) apart. They can be harvested from autumn onwards. Calabrese broccoli is planted out in early summer for a mid- to late summer crop: cut the main head on each plant first to encourage plenty of smaller heads to grow on side shoots.

Good varieties For autumn and winter cabbage: 'Minicole' or 'Celtic'; for winter only: 'January King'; calabrese broccoli: 'Green Comet', 'Jewel'.

Salad crops
Quick-maturing salad crops such as spring onions, lettuce and saladini (a mixture of various salad leaves) can be sown in shallow drills. Ideally sow at three-weekly intervals, to ensure a succession throughout the summer rather than a glut. Thinning out the seedlings and transplanting some of the thinnings also means those lettuces will be ready a week or two later than the

Left: Stake outdoor tomatoes as they grow to support the plants firmly and ensure a good crop.

Below: You can see why the plants really needed staking, given the weight of the crop.

ones left in the original drills. Alternatively, grow 'cut-and-come-again' crops such as loose-leaf lettuce and saladini where you pick the leaves only as you want them and leave the plants growing in the soil to produce more. Lamb's lettuce (or corn-salad) and rocket are both easy 'cut-and-come-again' salad crops which are expensive to buy and which taste much better freshly picked.

Good varieties Lettuce: 'Lollo Biondo', 'Lollo Rosso', 'Action'.

THE LEGUME BED

Again, add compost at the usual rate to the legume bed and fork it in lightly.

Runner beans

For runner beans, you need to prepare a bean trench ahead of time – in the winter, if possible,

Right: A veritable cornucopia – a selection of produce from our organic garden.

but at least one month before planting out the beans. Dig a trench about one spade's depth and one spade's width, then spread any kitchen waste, such as fruit and vegetable peelings, in the bottom. Cover it with soil and leave it to rot down. By the time you come to plant, it will have broken down into good organic matter, which beans, being very greedy feeders, will enjoy.

Ideally make two trenches with enough space between them so that the rows of canes can go inside the trenches. When the beans are grow-

Right: Runner beans are attractive climbers for any part of the garden.

Below: The peas are already scrambling well up their pea-sticks, while the bronze-leafed lettuces look almost too good to eat.

ing, they will not then be sheltering the trenches from valuable rain. If possible, make the trenches run east–west rather than north–south, because that way the beans don't create too much shade for the vegetables around them.

While you can sow runner beans directly into the soil about two weeks before the usual time of the last frosts in your area, the best way is to start them off in boxes in late April/early May, keep them in a frost-free place and plant them out once all danger of frost is past. You can use any box, even a stout cardboard one, and grow them in ordinary garden soil. They don't need compost and are vigorous enough to cope with any weeds that may germinate in the box with them. Keep the box in the shed, the garage or even an unheated bedroom covered with a sheet of glass and newspaper. Remove once the first beans have germinated and keep them well watered until they are ready to go outside.

Set up a double row of bean poles or bamboo canes over the trench you prepared earlier, allowing 30cm (1ft) between canes and 60cm (2ft) between rows, and plant one bean plant at the base of each cane. Alternatively, if you're growing them in a border, put in a wigwam of six or eight canes, or even grow them on fences with ornamental climbers. They were originally introduced to this country as ornamental plants, and many years later people realized that their seed pods could be eaten.

The plants will already be starting to twine, so simply help them towards the canes and let them get on with it. Once they are planted, water them thoroughly and if possible mulch with organic matter to conserve the moisture in the soil. They do need plenty of water – about 4 litres per square metre (just under 1 gallon per square yard) every day – so don't let them dry out. Once they have reached the top of the canes, you can pinch out the growing tip or leave it. They will reach about 2.8m (9ft) in all. Start cropping as soon as the beans are 15cm (6in) or so long. They become tough and stringy if you let

them get much bigger. Harvest them regularly – every other day at the height of the season – to encourage them to continue producing. If you go on holiday, persuade a neighbour to carry on picking the beans while you're away, so that your plants will still be cropping when you get home. At the end of the season, leave a few pods to grow and mature and use the beans for next year's seed.

Good varieties 'Painted Lady', 'Polestar'.

Peas

To sow peas, make shallow flat-bottomed drills about 15cm (6in) wide and 30cm (1ft) apart and sow the seed in rows three abreast, allowing 5cm (2in) between each seed. Cover them with soil, taking care not to disturb them. The main pest of peas is mice, which will eat the lot given the chance, so protect your crop with a tunnel of fine chicken wire pushed well into the soil at the sides and ends. As soon as the peas have germinated, remove the wire and push twiggy hazel sticks into the rows for the plants to climb. The sooner the peas start to climb, the heavier the crop will be.

In cold areas, if you have a greenhouse or unheated porch, sow your peas in compost in a length of plastic guttering. Once they are about 8cm (3in) high, dig a shallow drill of roughly the same dimensions as the length of guttering. Then carefully slide the contents of the guttering straight into the drill.

Pea moth is the other main pest of this crop. Its small creamy caterpillars are the maggots you find inside pea pods. It lays its eggs on flowering pea plants between June and mid-August, and tiny caterpillars find their way into the developing pods and feed on the peas as they grow. One way to defeat the menace is to sow early varieties of peas in February, so that the flowering period is over before the moth is active. If you have to sow later, cover the peas with fine mesh or fleece before they start to flower. Harvest peas when pods have begun to swell. Pick mangetout types when the pods are about 7.5 cm (3 in) long and still flat.

Once cropping is over, cut off the foliage and put it on the compost heap but leave the roots in place to release their nitrogen into the soil, ready for the brassicas next year. Alternatively, sow green manure (see page 84).

Good varieties Earlies: 'Early Onward', maincrop: 'Senator'; mangetout: 'Sugar Snap'.

Onions

The easiest way to produce a crop of onions is to grow them from sets – very small onion bulbs. Dig over the soil so that it is loose enough just to push the sets in, and space them 5cm (2in) apart. This way you'll produce medium-sized onions rather than enormous ones, but then most families use only a medium-sized onion at a time. Discard any sets that feel soft when you squeeze them or any that have already started sprouting. Cover them with soil so that the neck of the onion is just showing above the surface. If you leave too much showing, the birds will pull them out, just for the fun of it. Should that happen, don't just push the bulb back down again, or you may damage the roots. Instead, dig it up carefully and replant it.

Good varieties: 'Jet Set', 'Red Supreme'

Sowing seeds in modules

Sowing some crops in modules is an easy and trouble-free way of getting them started. Modules are better than pots or seed trays, because when it is time to plant out the young plants, you simply push them out with the block of compost in which they are growing so that there is no disturbance to the roots.

Start by filling the tray of modules with compost and pressing it lightly down to fill each one to the brim. Then, using the special tamper that comes with the trays, make shallow depressions in each

one. Sprinkle no more than two or three seeds in each module. If all of them germinate, remove the weakest, leaving the strongest to grow on.

If you are sowing more than one crop in a tray of modules, always work from left to right and up each row, rather than up and down, so that you will always know where you are. Put in a label at the start of each new crop.

Once the seeds are all sown, cover with sieved compost. If you don't have a sieve, an old squash or tennis racket will do the job. Take a generous handful of compost and start rubbing it through before you reach the modules so you don't get the first, large amount swamping them. Carefully level off any excess with a plant label, ruler, or any handy straight edge.

The best way to water is from beneath, so that the seeds are pulled down into the compost and not washed out. Stand the trays in a few centimetres of water and as soon as the surface of the compost is moist, remove them and let them drain. Remove the plant labels, carefully laying them down in the right order, cover the tray with clingfilm to keep the moisture in and then carefully push the labels back in through it, taking care not to tear the clingfilm more than is necessary.

Stand the trays inside on a sunny windowsill and keep a close eye on them. Since seedlings will grow towards the light, give the trays a quarter-turn every day or so to keep them growing as straight as possible. As soon as the first seeds have germinated, take off the clingfilm.

Thin the seedlings, removing all but the strongest one. It may seem cruel but it is the only way to ensure healthy crops. In late spring/early summer, start hardening them off by taking them outside in the daytime and bringing them in again at night. After a week or so, provided no frost is forecast, leave them out at night. Then they are ready to plant out. Push each block of compost, plus young plant, carefully out of its module from underneath and plant the whole lot in the appropriate bed in the vegetable garden.

FRUIT

Above and below: Technically speaking, the Turk's Turban gourds which are growing over the arch are fruits. Their spectacular leaves and rapid growth are also very valuable for filling space in a newly planted garden.

Left: The old damson tree in the corner, laden with fruit, makes a big contribution to our fruit and vegetable garden.

In recent years there has been a trend away from growing fruit, largely because modern gardens tend to be small and fruit can take up a lot of space. However, it really doesn't have to, and if you have a wall or fence, you can grow apples, pears, cherries, peaches, plums, gooseberries, blackberries and redcurrants trained against it, where they take up less ground space than a hedge.

In our organic garden we divided the fruit and vegetable area from the rest of the garden with a screen of espaliered pears – 'Williams' and 'Doyenné du Comice' planted in October, the ideal time for planting fruit trees, and trained against wires stretched taut between upright angle irons.

You can buy a wide range of fruit trees bearing familiar names, such as 'Granny Smith' apples and 'Morello' cherries, grafted on to what are called 'dwarfing rootstocks' which ensure that the trees always stay small, and trained in a variety of ways to grow flat. There are cordons (a single stem grown at 45 degrees), espaliers (which have three or four pairs of branches growing out sideways from the main stem), step-over trees (which are in fact one-tier espaliers, grown low enough to step over) and fan-trained trees (which, as the name suggests, have branches fanning outwards from the main stem). You can train the trees yourself, which is the cheapest way of doing it. It is easier, especially for beginners, though, to buy two- or three-year-old trees whose training is well under way.

Many varieties of apples and pears need another variety grown close by to ensure successful pollination, so you'll need to choose varieties that flower at the same time. They are grouped as early-, mid- or late-flowering. There are even 'family trees' of apples and pears, on which three different varieties that flower at the same time, such as 'James Grieve', 'Spartan' and 'Cox's Orange Pippin', are grafted on to a single rootstock. These are available as fan-trained trees as well.

Pruning trained fruit is simpler than you may

think. With apple and pear trees more than one year old, prune in late summer, cutting back all shoots growing directly from the main stems to 7.5cm (3in) and any shoots coming off those side shoots to 2.5cm (1in). That way you will build up a framework of 'spurs' on which the fruit will be borne. When the cordon's, or espalier's, leading shoot has reached the top of the wall or wire frame, cut it out. You may well see a few varieties of apples and pears described as 'tip bearers' – bearing the fruit at the tip of the shoot, rather than on spurs – and while the pruning method is slightly different, they will come to no harm if you prune them all the same way.

With plums, apricots and sweet cherries, you prune twice. First, in summer, pinch out any shoots growing into or directly away from the wall, and shorten the remaining shoots to six or seven leaves. In autumn, after you have picked the fruit, shorten the shoots by half. Do the same every year.

Peaches, nectarines and sour cherries such as 'Morello' fruit on last year's wood, so need different treatment. In spring rub out any shoots that are growing in the wrong direction, and then in summer look for shoots made last year and shorten them to four or five leaves. Once you have picked the fruit in autumn, shorten those shoots back to the two lowest shoots and tie them in; they will be next year's fruiting wood.

Like many mature gardens, Jani's and Rob's already had a pair of splendid apple trees – a 'Bramley's Seedling' (the best cooking apple) and a 'James Grieve' (an eater with an excellent flavour, not unlike a Cox). They functioned as climbing frame, swing and hammock support, too. There was also a damson at the far end of the garden. All three were in reasonably good shape, though they had not been pruned for some considerable time.

> *It's important when pruning to make clean cuts, since jagged messy ones encourage diseases to take hold*

Renovating old fruit trees

The damson had cropped heavily two years previously, had produced only about half a dozen fruits last year, but was heavily laden this year. Like all members of the plum family, it flowers early, and so is vulnerable to late frosts. That was probably the explanation for the poor crop last year. Although it had been well pruned in the past and had a good open centre to allow air to circulate freely and prevent fungal diseases such as mildew, it was weighing down on the fruit cage and casting too much shade on the ground beneath.

Like all plums, damsons are best pruned in early summer so that they grow away very quickly from the wound, otherwise they are vulnerable to silverleaf, a disease which enters the plant through damaged tissue, causing the leaves to turn a silvery colour and the branch to start dying off. Pruning in the summer also helps restrict other new growth, so that the tree can devote all its energies to ripening the fruit. Pruning of other fruit trees such as pears and apples in late winter, however, helps to stimulate new growth.

As with any task, having the right tools for the job makes life easier. It's important when pruning to make clean cuts, since jagged messy ones encourage diseases to take hold, so you'll need sharp secateurs. For the thicker branches you'll need a pruning saw – the folding ones are not expensive and do a remarkably good job. If you can lay your hands on a pair of loppers, too, so much the better.

Remove branches thin enough for the secateurs to cut cleanly as close to the main branch as possible. Don't leave jagged or stubby ends because they are open to disease and are likely to die back into the tree. With a larger heavier branch, lop off most of it, leaving a stump of about 30cm (1ft), and then take that off flush with the main branch or trunk with the pruning saw. Make a cut underneath the branch first, then saw down from the top. Without the lower cut, there is a danger that, when you have almost sawn right through it, the weight of the branch may pull it away from the tree, tearing the bark underneath in the process and again leaving the tree open to disease.

Here are some guidelines for pruning neglected trees:

1 As with all pruning, the first thing to do is assess the tree and see what needs to be removed for practical reasons – the tree is now too big for its space, for example, or the growth is causing problems. Prune sensitively to maintain the overall shape of the tree where possible, and keep standing back and looking at what you have done, rather than get carried away and take off too much in any one place.

2 Next look for and prune out any dead wood and any that is diseased, spindly or unproductive. Do not prune watershoots – very sappy, green growths which appear from older pruning wounds. These should be torn off, in the same way that suckers on roses are pulled off to prevent regrowth. Keep an eye on the tree, and should any

---

Fruit for a small garden

Apples
Mid-season flowering:
'Discovery', 'Fiesta' and Katy'
Mid- to Late-season flowering:
'Gala', 'Pixie' and 'Winston'

Blackcurrants
'Ben Sarek', 'Ben Tirran'

Figs
'Brown Turkey'

Gooseberries
'Invicta' or
'Whinham's Industry'

Pears
'Williams', 'Doyenné du Comice' and 'Merton Pride'

Raspberries
'Autumn Bliss', 'Malling Promise' or
'Glen Prosen'

Redcurrants
'Red Lake' or 'Junifer'

Strawberries
'Elsanta' or 'Honeoye'

---

new watershoots form, rub them out as soon as you see them.

3 As a general rule, horizontal branches are more productive than vertical ones, so you want to encourage the former and remove the latter. As with roses, what you are aiming for is an open goblet shape, so if the centre of the tree is congested, prune out the smaller branches growing straight up from the main branches.

4 Neglected trees are probably starving too, so clear all the weeds from the soil around the base of the tree – a circle about a metre across should be enough – and spread on a layer of compost or well-rotted manure at the usual rate (two spadesful of compost or one of manure) and water well. Make a circular wall of soil about 10cm (4in) high around the compost and water inside that. This keeps the water where you want it – over the tree's root system – so that it can filter slowly down and be taken up by the tree, rather than running everywhere and going to waste.

5 In subsequent years keep an eye on the tree, and if it seems to be producing too much small fruit, reduce the spurs by taking out the weaker ones and any on the undersides of branches. You may find that your fruit tree produces a heavy crop one year, and a very small one the next, despite your efforts. Don't worry – some fruit trees are just like that.

Left: Early september. There's a bumper crop on the old damson tree this year which is just about ready for picking.

Far right: By early September 'James Grieve' is covered in bright red apples, almost ready for harvesting.

Right: Make the most of available space by training soft fruit such as redcurrants against a fence. You can train them as cordons, or fans.

Below: The first autumn-fruiting raspberries.

Below: Strawberries produce 'runners' – basically new plants at the end of long stems. Peg them down into the soil, so that they can root. When they have, cut them away from the parent plant.

Soft fruit

Even very small gardens have room for some soft fruit, though it may be only a couple of strawberry plants, but given that the birds enjoy soft fruit as much as we do, the best way to grow it is out of beak's reach, in a fruit cage. In our fruit and vegetable plot the obvious place was in the opposite corner to that occupied by the damson tree. We ordered the size we wanted by mail order and Rob and Jani managed to put it together in a few hours with the minimum of cursing and swearing.

We decided to grow raspberries – summer-fruiting and autumn-fruiting – gooseberries, blackcurrants, redcurrants and strawberries.

All soft fruit benefits from an application of organic fertilizers before planting, except strawberries which are inclined to produce more leaf than fruit on soil that is too rich.

The main elements needed are nitrogen (N) for leaf growth, phosphorus (P) for root development and potassium or potash (K) for fruit and flowers. 'N for shoots, P for roots and K for fruits' is an easy way to remember it. Add hoof and horn for nitrogen at the rate of 125g per square metre (4oz per square yard), rock phosphate, a good source of phosphorus, at the rate of 250g per square metre (8oz per square yard) or 65g per square metre (2.5 oz per square yard) of seaweed meal. Well-rotted garden compost is also a very good source.

In the first year, when the aim is to get the plants established and growing strongly, however, you don't want to encourage flowering and fruiting, so there is no need to give them any potash. In subsequent years, unless the soil is seriously depleted in potash, spreading hay or straw on the soil around the base of the plants will provide all they need. If you do need to boost the potash, add either bonemeal at the rate of 75g per square metre (3oz per square yard) or rock potash at the rate of 125g (4oz). Although all bonemeal, which is made from the ground bones of animals, is sterilized to destroy anthrax and scrapie, BSE can remain so it is worth wearing gloves when you apply it. Alternatively, mulch the fruit with comfrey leaves, which are rich in potash.

RASPBERRIES

Raspberries are best trained on rows of wires about 60cm (2ft) apart, stretched between pairs of wooden posts about 1.8m (6ft) high.

Dig a trench about 30cm (1ft) wide and deep, and since they like rich fertile soil, work manure (one spadeful to the square metre) into the earth at the bottom. Raspberries are greedy feeders, so if the soil is depleted you need to add some organic fertilizers too.

Plant the raspberries 45cm (18in) apart, just a little lower than they were growing in their pots, to encourage plenty of bushy growth from below ground level. If you plant in autumn, cut the canes down to 15cm (6in) from the ground so that the plant can put all its energies into establishing a strong root system and new bushy growth. If you plant pot-grown plants in spring, you may find that the old canes have already been cut back by the grower and any growth is new season's. Since summer raspberries fruit on canes that are one year old, this new growth will produce next summer's fruit. Autumn-fruiting kinds, though, will bear fruit on this year's canes, so you should get a small crop on them.

As the canes grow, tie them to the wires, spacing them about 10cm (4in) apart. Once the canes have reached about 8cm (3in) above the top wire, cut them off.

After the canes have borne fruit, cut them out completely, right down to ground level, and tie in the new canes, produced that summer, to take their place. With autumn-fruiting raspberries, simply cut them right back to ground level in late winter.

Good varieties Early: 'Malling Promise', Mid-season: 'Malling Jewel', 'Glen Prosen', 'Julia'; autumn-fruiting: 'Autumn Bliss'.

GOOSEBERRIES

To make the best use of space within a small fruit cage, try training gooseberries as espaliers, single, double or triple cordons. Not only does training them flat against wires reduce the space they take up, but it also encourages them to fruit more heavily and, by keeping the centre of the bush open, discourages American gooseberry mildew.

Good varieties 'Invicta' (has the best resistance to gooseberry mildew), 'Whinham's Industry'.

BLACKCURRANTS

Blackcurrants are perhaps the greediest soft fruit of all, so prepare the planting hole well with manure at the usual rate, as well as with organic fertilizers. If you plant bare-rooted bushes in autumn, plant them about 5cm (2in) deeper than the soil mark on the stem to encourage new shoots to emerge from below the soil and then cut the existing growth back hard. If you plant container-grown fruit in spring, you can assume that they will have been cut back the previous autumn, so what you now have is the new season's growth.

Since blackcurrants bear most fruit on wood produced the previous year, you will not get much of a crop in the first year, nor will the bushes need pruning. With older bushes, the secret of success once they are established is to prune out between a quarter and a third of the old wood, which has borne fruit, right down to soil level every autumn to ensure that there is always strong new growth. Over three or four years you will have renewed the bush completely.

Good varieties 'Ben Lomond', 'Ben Tirran'; 'Ben Sarek' (for small spaces).

REDCURRANTS AND WHITECURRANTS

Just to confuse you, redcurrants and whitecurrants are grown in the same way as gooseberries, not as blackcurrants, and respond well to training. Grow them as cordons, single, double or triple, or fan-train them. Choose a bush with three strong shoots – one on either side of the central stem. Tie each side shoot to a bamboo cane and tie it at 45 degrees to horizontal wires on the fence. Reduce these arms to about 40cm (16in) and prune out the central stem right down to the fork to encourage new shoots to grow out of the point where the central stem and each side shoot meet. As they develop over the summer, tie in the two strongest shoots above each arm, and one below to form more arms of the fan, and remove the rest. Cut the stems back again in early spring the following year, thin the new shoots to about 10cm (4in) apart in early summer and in midsummer tie in the remaining new shoots to fill out the fan shape.

Good varieties Red: 'Red Lake', 'Laxton's No. 1', 'Junifer'; white: 'White Versailles'.

STRAWBERRIES

Strawberries do best in free-draining soil and in a sunny spot. If yours is heavy soil, dig in plenty of soil conditioner – not compost – to improve the drainage. Unless the soil is very low in nutrients, don't add nutrients because the plants will then produce a lot of leaf at the expense of flowers and therefore fruit. Ideally, plant strawberries in late summer or autumn to produce fruit next year, though you can plant them in spring. Strictly speaking, you should pick off all the flowers as they form in the first season, so that all the plants' energies can go into getting established rather than in bearing fruit, but you can leave one or two just to give you a little instant gratification in experiencing the thrill of picking your own strawberries this year.

Once the fruits begin to form, spread a layer of straw underneath them. This keeps the berries off the soil so they stay clean, but it can make a slug problem worse. After you have harvested the berries, cut off all the old leaves with shears, leaving just the crown of the plant – the central tuft of new leaves – and add any straw and old foliage to the compost heap. In subsequent years, peg down 'runners' to root into the soil and form new plants to replace the old ones.

Good varieties 'Honeoye', 'Elsanta', 'Aromel'.

SOIL AND HOW TO TREAT IT

Above: Improving your soil before you plant pays obvious dividends, with healthy, free-flowering plants.

All good gardeners, whether they are organic or not, know that a fertile soil is the key to success in creating a flourishing garden. Gardeners make much greater demands on the soil than nature itself does, and so we have to put back into it the goodness which the plants take out in order to grow. Perhaps the difference between the organic and non-organic gardener in this respect is that the former relies entirely on the soil to produce healthy growth and will feed the soil rather than the plants, while the latter will feed the plants too with additional inorganic fertilizers such as rose fertilizer, Growmore, or proprietary liquid feeds such as Phostrogen or Miracle-Gro. While it's true, as non-organic gardeners will tell you, that plants cannot tell the difference between organic and inorganic nutrients, inorganic fertilizers can build up in the soil, leach through to the water table and add to the problems of nitrates and so forth in our water.

Without a doubt the best way to increase the fertility of the soil is to add organic matter, which simply means anything that once was alive, is now dead and that has rotted down to form a bulky residue. This includes vegetable waste of every kind – kitchen scraps such as potato peelings, apple cores, lawn mowings, soft prunings (woody ones take too long to break down unless shredded), top growth of vegetables and annuals at the end of the summer, even annual weeds that are not in flower or have not set seed, newspaper, bark – all of which breaks down into garden compost. It also includes well-

1 *Comfrey (Symphytum) liquid makes an excellent organic fertilizer. The very best variety to grow for the purpose is S. 'Bocking 14', but any comfrey will provide some valuable liquid fertilizer.*

2 *Fix a length of plastic drainpipe, sealed at the bottom with a cap and nozzle, to a wall or fence and push comfrey leaves into the top.*

3 *Use a plastic bottle filled with water as a weight to press the leaves down firmly inside the pipe.*

4 *In a week or so, comfrey liquid will start to drip out of the nozzle at the bottom and into the plastic container.*

Left: Opening up a sticky clay soil with organic matter and grit enables you to grow plants that need free-draining soil, like sedum and perovskia.

rotted farmyard manure – which started life as grass or hay before passing through the horses, cows or sheep. You can tell when organic matter is well-rotted because it is a rich dark brown colour, has a crumbly texture with no recognizable lumps, and, most important, doesn't smell.

The reason it has to be well-rotted before it can be usefully applied to the soil is that, as it breaks down, the bacteria doing the job extract valuable nitrogen from the soil and in the process deprive the plants of it. On the rare occasion when you do add neat kitchen waste to the soil – if you're preparing a trench for runner beans ahead of time, for example – the material has finished breaking down before the plants go in.

Making compost

Home-made compost is not only one of the best soil improvers you can get, it is also a very environmentally sound way of disposing of garden rubbish that would otherwise add to the mountains of garbage we produce and which has to be disposed of either in landfill sites or in giant incinerators. To be fair, some local authorities have started composting schemes, under which you can deliver your green waste to a special dump where it is turned into compost and sold back to you at a very low cost.

If you follow just a few simple rules, though, and follow them faithfully, it really isn't difficult to turn your kitchen and garden waste into brown gold.

To make good compost you need a number of elements. First, you need air circulating through it, so don't ever cram the raw material into the bin too tightly, and always mix fine waste such as grass cuttings with chunkier waste like cabbage leaves, big weeds, torn-up newspaper or thoroughly soaked straw. Grass cuttings on their own will turn to sour-smelling slime. With 'hot compost', it's also important to empty the bin a couple of times during the process, give every-

thing a good stir round to add more air and then pile it all back in again. Second, you need bacteria to break down the green waste, and given that there are millions in every crumb of soil, you'll be adding all you need on the roots of the old plants you are composting.

To feed the bacteria, you need nitrogen. If you have the correct balance of material in the heap, you shouldn't need to add any extra. If you don't, add seaweed meal, or organic compost activator. Urine is another good activator and some organic gardeners – male, of course – are known to recycle beer, cider and other liquids they have consumed straight on to the heap.

Next, you need water. There will probably be enough moisture in the green waste you put in, but if it is very dry, damp it well with the hose, or, if you use straw, soak it thoroughly first. In very hot weather the heap may dry out round the edges and so those areas won't rot down unless you water them. On the other hand you don't want the heap to get sodden, because that too slows down the rotting process, so cover it in winter to keep out the rain.

Heat is important, primarily to speed the whole process, and the centre of a well-managed compost heap gets remarkably hot. When you are starting compost from scratch, and adding material a little at a time, very little heat will be generated, but all that means is the compost will take longer to break down. Keep the compost warm by choosing a bin with sides that are solid, except for a few air holes in the case of non-porous plastic ones, and by covering it. You can use black polythene, which also helps keep the rain off, but old carpet or something similar is preferable since it allows air in.

COMPOST BINS

Ideally you should have two compost bins, side by side, so that you can be using the finished compost from one while you are still making compost in the other. There is a wide range of bins on the market, made from plastic or wood.

Look for one with no bottom, and with more or less solid sides. Avoid the wooden kinds with large gaps between the planks since the waste will just dry out before it has a chance to start rotting. For the same reason, mesh bins are not a good idea unless you line them with thick cardboard or many layers of newspaper first.

Alternatively make your own wooden bins, as we did. Those we made are called New Zealand bins, with planks that slide out at the front to let you get at your compost easily. As long as you can wield a hammer, they really aren't that difficult to make.

To construct a bin 1 cubic metre in volume, start by making one of the side panels. Nail 1m (3ft) lengths of planking – old floorboards will do – to two 2 x 4in uprights 1m (3ft) long, leaving a very small gap between them to allow air in. When you have made the two side panels, nail the third set of planks forming the back to the existing uprights. To make the front, nail two battens to each of the inner sides of the front uprights, wide enough apart for the front planks to slide up and down between them.

Though functional, compost bins don't have to look ugly, so stain them with an organic woodstain. We used a lovely rich blue, but there are other good colours available. To keep the compost bin together when it is full, either use a piece of timber with notches cut at each end to fit on to the top plank on either side or, more basic, use a piece of stout string to tie round the top of the two front uprights.

If at all possible, site your compost bins directly on the soil rather than on a hard surface. It will aid the composting process and eventually you'll even get earthworms wriggling up through the heap and producing the finest compost of all – earthworm-digested.

In a *very* small town garden, you may have so little room that, rather than give up even one precious square metre of ground space to a compost bin, it makes more sense to grow plants in it, and buy the small amounts of compost you need.

RECIPE FOR COMPOST

If you can fill one bin with green waste right away, you can make a 'hot' compost and will get results that much quicker, so collect up as much kitchen and garden waste as you can lay your hands on. Your neighbours and the local greengrocers will probably think you are mad if you ask for theirs too, but will probably be glad to get rid of it. As long as you include plenty of soft, sappy material in the mix, you won't need any compost activator.

Make the first layer of coarse waste – cabbage leaves, big weeds, straw or newspaper – to ensure that you get air into the bottom of the heap. Then add a layer of grass cuttings – between 10 and 15cm (4 and 6in) – mixed in with a generous layer of coarser waste, followed by straw. Then add another layer of grass cuttings and soft, sappy, green waste, mixed with coarser waste, more straw topped with grass cuttings, perhaps mixed with shredded newspaper this time, and so on until you reach the top of the bin. You'll be surprised how quickly it shrinks as it starts to break down, leaving more room on the top to add further layers.

After a few weeks, the heap will have heated up and started to cool down again, because it has exhausted most of the air. To incorporate more air, tip all the compost out – easily done with a homemade bin like ours, since you just slide up the front planks and pull it out. Toss it around with a fork and, having replaced the front planks, pile it loosely back into the bin and cover it again. Mixing it up will also draw in the material from the sides of the heap which will be composting more slowly than that in the centre. Don't add new material at this stage, since it will obviously delay the breaking-down process. Repeat the process a few weeks later after the compost has heated up and cooled down again. Depending on the material you use and the weather, you should have usable compost in two or three months in summer, while a heap made in the autumn should give you compost by the following spring.

If you can't fill one bin all in one go, you can make 'cold' compost. It still heats up, and breaks down, but takes much longer to do so. Add waste as you collect it, though do make sure you mix coarse with fine.

Avoid adding cooked kitchen waste or meat to compost bins since it attracts vermin, and don't add any pernicious perennial weeds, such as couch grass, bindweed or ground elder, any annual weeds that are either flowering or setting seed, or any diseased plants.

While some diseases may be killed off by the composting process, so much depends on the

Above and right: New Zealand bins are very simple to make if you can wield a hammer, and the sliding panels in the front make them very simple to use. Stain them with an organic woodstain – they can be beautiful as well as functional.

Right: Fennel and Aster x frikartii 'Mönch'.

temperature reached that it is impossible to say with any certainty what's safe and what isn't. It's best not to add woody prunings unless you can shred them first because they take such a long time to properly break down. Equally with really tough stems such as cabbage stalks, it's a good idea to smash them with a hammer first to help them break down more quickly.

WORM COMPOST

There is no doubt that worm compost is very good stuff because it is so fine, but, to be honest, managing a wormery successfully, whether it's one you build yourself or one that you buy, is a bit tricky. For a start, you must add only small amounts of kitchen waste at a time – a maximum of 7.5cm (3in) a week – and the special

*Right: A healthy soil produces healthy growth,
of ornamental plants as well as edible ones.*

brandling or tiger worms need to be kept above
a certain temperature all winter, ideally above
7°C (45°F), or they will die, which means bringing the bin under cover and insulating it.

Leaf mould

Although leaf mould has very little nutritional value, it is a wonderful soil conditioner, both for clay soil, to improve the texture and the drainage, and for sandy soil, to help make it more moisture-retentive. It is also an important element in home-made potting compost.

To make leaf mould, you'll need a simple bin about 1 cubic metre in size, made from a wooden frame and chicken wire. Unlike green waste, which is broken down by bacteria, leaves are broken down by fungi which need more light and less heat. Leaves take a long time to rot down – at least a year and sometimes two, while tough leaves such as chestnut and plane will take three years or more.

In autumn collect leaves from your garden and anywhere else you can find them, though be aware that those lying beside busy roads will be contaminated with lead. If you have a shredder, put the leaves through it first, which will speed up the rotting process considerably. Alternatively, if you have a mower with a collecting bag, spread the leaves on the lawn so that you can mow over them, chopping them up and collecting them in one go. Pile the leaves into the container and bang them down hard with the back of a rake or, better still, if possible climb in and trample them down. They need to be damp, so if they are bone dry when you put them into the bin, give them a good watering and in very dry weather give them another wetting with the hose.

Green manure

Green manure crops are those which are grown purely to be dug back into the soil to increase its fertility. It can be done on a large scale in a garden where the soil is very poor, or on a smaller scale in the vegetable garden, following on crops which mature in early or mid-summer. They have the added benefit of keeping the soil covered – an important principle of organic gardening – and their roots help aerate the soil. The best crop for this purpose is grazing rye (*Secale cereale*), sown in late summer and dug in as close as possible to planting time the following spring. Don't sow it in the bed where crops such as carrots are to be grown from seed the following year, since it produces a chemical which inhibits germination. *Phacelia tanacetifolia*, a pretty blue-flowered annual, is also a good green manure crop but isn't totally hardy, so in cold areas it's best sown in early summer and dug in about eight weeks later. Mustard and lupins are often recommended for green manure, but since they are each related to commonly grown vegetable crops – the former to brassicas and the latter to legumes – it's better to avoid them in most vegetable gardens.

Loam pile

If you have to strip turf from any part of your garden, don't throw it into the skip, because what you have removed is a very valuable resource. You can use it upside down in planting holes to provide valuable moisture-retentive organic matter for the new plants as it rots down, or you can make a loam pile with it.

Stack the turf, grass side down, in an out-of-the-way corner of the garden and cover it with black polythene or, dare I say it, old carpet, to exclude the light and stop it from becoming too wet. This kills off the grass and allows it to break down into the soil, producing a crumbly loam, rich in nutrients, by the following year. Mixed with leaf mould – two bucketsful of loam to one of leaf mould – it makes perfect compost for containers. Ideally you should sterilize the loam first to kill off any weed seeds and diseases. Either use a small soil sterilizer, though these are hard to find, or a domestic oven at 80°C (176°F) for 30 minutes (place it on a baking tray covered with foil) or even use a microwave (900g [2lb] of soil needs two and a half minutes at full power). It has to be said it is a rather smelly, messy business, so it may be preferable to put up with a few weeds in your potting compost.

Organic fertilizers

There is a vast array of organic fertilizers on the market, some general, some specific.

Three good general fertilizers are blood, fish and bone, seaweed meal, and pelleted chicken manure. Blood, fish and bone contains the three main nutrients – nitrogen (for shoots), which is quickly released, phosphorus (for roots) and potassium or potash (for fruits), which are released more slowly. Seaweed meal also contains trace elements which makes it a better all-round fertilizer, but it is much more expensive. Calcified seaweed is cheaper and contains the same nutrients and trace elements but makes soil limey. Pelleted chicken manure is a popular organic general fertilizer whose pelleted form means that it releases its nutrients fairly slowly.

For nitrogen, hoof and horn is a good slow-release product, while dried blood is the opposite and has a fast tonic effect. Good sources of phosphorus are bonemeal and rock phosphate, while rock potash is, not surprisingly, rich in potassium. These fertilizers, which come in a dry form, are either hoed lightly into the surface of the soil or are mixed in with the soil at planting time.

Liquid fertilizers, such as liquid seaweed, can be watered on to the soil around the roots of the plants or given as a foliar feed – sprayed on to the leaves for a quick tonic effect.

HOME-MADE LIQUID FERTILIZERS

One of the best liquid feeds is liquid manure, which is made by half-filling a sack with manure and submerging it in a barrel of water for a few weeks. When the water is rich brown and, it must be said, distinctly pongy, remove the sack and dump the wet manure on to the compost heap.

You will then have enough liquid manure to last you a year. To prevent GBH of the olfactory nerves and deteriorating relations with your neighbours, do keep the barrel tightly covered. Use its contents neat on the soil, but only when the soil is wet, otherwise it will scorch the plants' roots, or dilute it by half and use it as a foliar feed.

Comfrey (*Symphytum*) also makes a first-class liquid feed, rich in potash, and so ideal for greenhouse crops such as tomatoes and cucumbers and for container plants. Ideally use *Symphytum* 'Bocking 14', a specially bred variety which is particularly rich in nutrients and which comes into leaf so early that you should be able to harvest leaves four times in the season. Other comfrey is invasive, and not as rich in nutrients.

There are two methods of making the liquid. The first method involves soaking the leaves in a water-butt – 3kg (7lb) of comfrey to 90 litres (20 gallons) of water – for three or four weeks, and then straining it, and using the resulting liquid undiluted.

The second method is pressing. Stack the leaves in a plastic barrel with a tap in the side and weight them down with a stone slab. After two or three weeks the liquid will start to run out. As you would expect, it is more concentrated than the liquid produced by the first method, so dilute it with about 15 parts of water.

In very small gardens, where there isn't room for a barrel or even the need for so much fertilizer, make a comfrey tube instead. Take a length of plastic drainpipe and fix it to the shed or fence with brackets, so that the end is 30cm (1ft) or so above the ground. Fit a cap to the bottom, with a nozzle in it, and place a bucket or watering can underneath. Fill the pipe with comfrey leaves, pressed well down. To keep the pressure on, fill a bottle – glass or plastic – with water to make a weight, tie stout string round its neck so that you can remove it easily, and then push it into the top of the pipe. In eight to ten days the liquid will start dripping through the hole in the bottom into the bucket or can. Dilute it as described above.

Whether you garden organically or not, you will still find that your plants will be attacked from time to time by pests and diseases. One of the most obvious differences between organic gardening and the traditional way is that you don't reach for the chemicals at the first sign of trouble. In the way that holistic medicine treats the whole person and concentrates on promoting good health rather than on treating illness, so the organic way of gardening also works on the basis that prevention is better than cure.

In a real emergency there are a few fungicides and pesticides that organic gardeners use, chosen because they do the least possible damage to the environment and, just as important, they don't enter the food chain. They are based on natural ingredients such as derris and pyrethrum and are effective against aphids, red spider mite and caterpillars.

For fungus diseases, such as potato blight, blackspot and mildew on roses, apples and gooseberries, you can use sulphur or a mixture like Bordeaux mixture, based on copper sulphate. Take care with sulphur, though, as some plants are 'sulphur shy'. Spray a test shoot and if the leaves drop off within twenty-four hours or start turning yellow, don't use it on the rest of the plant.

There is no doubt, however, that well-grown, strong, healthy plants are far less likely to succumb to pests and diseases than their weaker brethren. So avoid over-watering and over-feeding because these produce just the kind of lush sappy growth that pests love. Avoid under-watering and under-feeding too, because that puts plants under stress of a different kind but leaves them equally open to pests and diseases. Mildew, for example, on ornamental plants and on gooseberries is exacerbated by dryness at the roots, so always keep them well watered, and also keep the latter well pruned to form an open goblet shape so that air can circulate freely and therefore help prevent mildew getting established.

Always thin seedlings out ruthlessly, even

though, if you are a new gardener, it is often heartbreaking to pull out and discard the majority of what comes up. Leave them too close together and they will be fighting for water, nutrients and light and as a result will be thin and spindly and, again, wide open to any diseases or pests that are around.

It's wise, too, to avoid monoculture – growing lots of the same type of plant in one place – because obviously, if the pests do find it, they will rapidly go through the entire crop. In small vegetable and fruit gardens like ours, however, there are not huge quantities of the same crops, so it should be less of a problem.

Eternal vigilance

Keep a very close eye on your plants, especially the edible ones, checking them every day if possible. That way you spot trouble as soon as it starts, rather than discovering too late that your crop is all but completely destroyed. Rubbing a few blackfly off your runner beans is relatively simple. Finding all the growing tips thickly encrusted and distorted as a result of their attentions is rather different.

Gooseberries can be devastated by gooseberry sawfly, the caterpillars of which munch their way through the leaves at an alarming rate, sometimes defoliating a bush entirely. While it won't kill the bush necessarily, it will seriously deplete next year's crop. So in April check low down or in the centre of the bush for eggs laid on the undersides of leaves. Pick them off and squash them. Check again, for caterpillars this

Above: Planting attractants such as convolvulus and tagetes in your vegetable garden will bring in beneficial insects such as ladybirds, lacewings and hoverflies to eat pests like aphids.

Right: Frogs, toads and hedgehogs are also invaluable allies in the war against pests like slugs, snails and caterpillars. Offering them shelter is a good way to attract them and get them to stay.

time, in early June, again in early July and in mid- to late August, since there can be several generations of caterpillars throughout the summer months. Pick them off and squash them or, if you are squeamish, spray with derris. Once you have seen your precious gooseberries savaged by this pest, you may find that your squeamishness disappears! Clear away any mulch round the base of the plant in case it harbours any over-wintering sawfly and if possible remove the roof of the fruit cage in winter to allow birds to clean up any eggs or grubs left in the soil.

Companion planting

The idea of companion planting – growing together plants which benefit each other in some way – as a means of keeping crops healthy is an appealing one. Most companion planting works by smell, either driving the pests away from the area because the fragrance is so strong – wormwood (*Artemisia*) is said to have this effect – or disguising the scent of the vulnerable plant with a stronger one so that the pest doesn't find its target. Ornamental onions (*Allium*) – chives and garlic, grown among roses, for instance – are said to ward off greenfly. Savory and other strongly aromatic herbs are believed to keep the aphids off beans, while the highly scented dwarf marigold (*Tagetes*) is meant to divert the cabbage white butterfly from your brassicas and is even said to keep eelworm away from potatoes.

Many gardeners swear by companion planting, but what scientific research there has been has not backed up most of these theories. While planting onions with carrots does seem to deter carrot fly, you need so many onions – at least three times the quantity of carrots – that it just isn't practical in a small garden.

Attracting help

Undoubtedly what does work very well is attractant planting – growing plants to attract the beneficial insects which eat pests. Beneficial insects include hoverflies, which look like anorexic wasps and of which there are forty-nine native species in the UK, lacewings, those delicate-looking insects with gauzy, pale green wings, and ladybirds, of which there are thirty-nine native species. Ladybirds lay their eggs directly into colonies of aphids and once the larvae hatch they make short work of these pests. Both the adults and their larvae – curious slate-grey creatures with very modern-looking orange markings, which are larger than the ladybirds they will become – devour vast quantities of aphids.

Hoverfly larvae are perhaps the most efficient aphid-eating machines – one larva can devour a whole aphid in about four minutes. Their other advantage is that, unlike ladybirds, they are not deterred by ants which seek to protect the aphids, since they farm them for their honeydew and even move them around plants to new leaves and buds from which they can suck the sap. Before the female hoverfly can lay her eggs, though, she needs to feed on pollen for the protein it contains. Since she has a short feeding tube, open-faced flowers with the pollen easily accessible are ideal. Easy-to-grow annuals such as the poached egg plant (*Limnanthes douglasii*), the dwarf morning glory (*Convolvulus tricolor*), nasturtiums (*Tropaeolum*), pot marigolds (*Calendula*) and the half-hardy annual French

> ❛ *Hoverfly larvae are perhaps the most efficient aphid-eating machines* ❜

marigold (*Tagetes*) are all good attractant plants. Not only are they functional, but they help to brighten up the vegetable garden as well.

Decoy or sacrificial planting is another variation on this theme, where you plant something the pest likes as much with the crop you want to protect. To protect potatoes from wireworm, grow rows of wheat on either side. The wireworms will attack the roots of the wheat before they start on the potatoes, so you can pull up the wheat plants and burn them. Alternatively stick pieces of potato or carrot on canes and bury them among the newly planted potatoes. Pull up the wireworm-infested pieces of vegetable from time to time, burn them and replace them with new ones. Neither method will eradicate the problem entirely, but it will help.

Other valuable pestivores need to be attracted to the vegetable garden in other ways. The ground beetle, which is black and shiny and about 1.5cm ($^2/_5$in) long, is also a valuable ally, eating eelworms, caterpillars, leatherjackets, cabbage root fly eggs and even slugs and snails. They feed at night, so they need somewhere damp and dark to hide during the day. Cover your soil with a mulch, or put down a few slates or flat stones under which they can hide.

Providing shelter is the best way of attracting hedgehogs too, which also eat slugs and snails, millipedes and other pests. You can feed them initially – dog food is much better for them than bread and milk, by the way – to encourage them

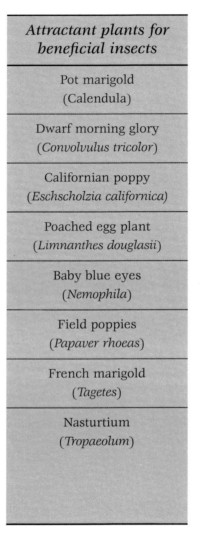

Attractant plants for beneficial insects

Pot marigold
(Calendula)

Dwarf morning glory
(*Convolvulus tricolor*)

Californian poppy
(*Eschscholzia californica*)

Poached egg plant
(*Limnanthes douglasii*)

Baby blue eyes
(*Nemophila*)

Field poppies
(*Papaver rhoeas*)

French marigold
(*Tagetes*)

Nasturtium
(*Tropaeolum*)

to stay, but obviously a hedgehog full of yummy Woof! is not going to make much impact on your pest population. A pile of logs, such as our Frog Hilton, will provide them with shelter – and always check your compost heap before you tip it out, and especially any unlit bonfire before you set light to it, to make sure they haven't set up home in there.

A pond will attract frogs and toads, which eat slugs in huge quantities, while toads also welcome cool damp shelter on dry land.

Birds are valuable allies, too, in controlling pests in your garden, though after they have pulled out your newly planted onion sets or stripped the fruit buds from your trees, you may feel that, with friends like these, who needs enemies? But they do do sterling work. Robins and wagtails eat caterpillars and raspberry beetle grubs, finches eat pests that live on buds, while thrushes of course make short work of snails. If slugs and snails are a real menace in your plot, help the thrushes along by laying planks in the vegetable garden at night, then turning them over in the morning, exposing the slugs and snails which have gathered there during the hours of darkness. Do make sure too that there is a handy stone nearby for the thrushes to use as an anvil for breaking snail shells.

Attract birds to your garden by providing food and shelter. Food can come from shrubs and herbaceous plants, not only native species, but their close relatives too. Make sure that you have some trees and

Above: Choose varieties that are disease-resistant. Unlike some Michalmas daisies, Aster frikartii *'Mönch' will not get mildew.*

shrubs that bear berries, such as cotoneaster, elder (*Sambucus*), the deciduous spindle (*Euonymus europaeus*), firethorn (*Pyracantha*), honeysuckle, rowan (*Sorbus*), hawthorn (*Crataegus*) and so on. Also grow plants such as cornflowers, Michaelmas daisies, scabious and sunflowers which produce seeds that the birds like, or in lean times, such as really cold spells in winter, feed them from the bird-table. A mixture of different foods – seeds, nuts, fat, bread – will attract a variety of different species of birds. If squirrels are a problem in your garden, use special wire mesh bird feeders to prevent them stealing the birds' food. Don't forget water – birds need to drink too, and so do insects such as butter-flies, which also take up the salts left behind when

water evaporates. In very cold weather put warm water out several times a day

As for shelter, berberis, hawthorn, holly, honey-suckle and the evergreen tassel bush (*Garrya elliptica*) all offer good nesting sites, while ivy makes one of the best of all for small birds (as well as pro-viding shelter for various over-wintering beneficial insects), so if you are going to prune it radically, do make sure that any fledglings have flown the nest before you start.

Left: Plastic bottles provide useful protection for young, tender seedlings against slugs and snails. Cutting the tops off not only allows more air in but also looks better.

Above: Horticultural mesh is the best protection against the attentions of the carrot fly.

Left: Mice are a major pest of peas. A piece of chicken wire pushed into the soil over them will keep them at bay.

Mechanical methods of warding off pests

Another good way of protecting plants is to create physical barriers against the pest concerned. Carrot fly is kept at bay by a tunnel of horticultural fleece (see page 65) while mice are kept off peas by chicken-wire tunnels until they have germinated. Pea moth strikes when the peas are in flower, so before the first flowers appear cover the plants with horticultural mesh.

Cabbage root fly, which attacks all members of the brassica family, is best dealt with by putting a mat around the stem of each cabbage plant, which prevents the female from getting up to the stem, inserting her egg tube next to it and laying her eggs. You can either buy the mats or make your own from spare carpet underlay. Cut pieces about 15cm (6in) square, then make slits from one side to the centre, where you also cut very small crosses. Slide each mat around the stem of the plant so that it fits very snugly – it must fit closely otherwise the female will still be able to get near enough to the stem to lay her eggs.

There are various barrier methods of deterring slugs and snails from plants. Any rough-textured mulch, such as coarse grit, cocoa shells or baked and crushed egg shells spread around the plant will help keep the surface crawlers away. Slugs tend to go for fresh young foliage, often destroying the plant entirely, so protect newly planted or germinated plants by cutting the top and bottom off plastic mineral water bottles with a sharp knife and sliding them over individual plants. You don't actually need to remove the tops, but the resulting plastic sleeves are far less obvious than a forest of bottles and your vegetable garden looks so much better if you do. Once the plants are growing strongly, and are able to cope with a degree of slug damage, remove the sleeves. You can also make slug 'pubs' – empty yogurt pots sunk into the soil every metre or so and filled with beer mixed with a little sugar. These need to be emptied regularly and refilled with beer.

Flea beetle is an irritating pest which attacks members of the cabbage family as well as nasturtiums and wallflowers, making hundreds of tiny holes in the leaves. They are small, black and shiny, and jump when disturbed, a characteristic which helps in their control. Take a piece of stiff card or hardboard and smear it with petroleum jelly or grease. Run it along just above the tops of the infested plants so that the draught lightly disturbs the leaves, making the beetles jump up and stick to the grease. Although damaged leaves look unsightly, the plant will recover.

The best way to trap earwigs, which do a lot of damage to ornamental plants, is to stuff flowerpots full of straw and place them upside down on canes among the susceptible plants. The earwigs crawl up the canes at dawn to hide during the day, so you can simply empty them out into a bucket of water in the morning.

To combat winter moth, a major pest of apples, use grease – either on a band of ready-impregnated paper tied round the trunk, or simply squirted onto it. You can buy both of these at most garden centres. The female moth is flightless and so crawls up the trunk to lay her eggs in the tree where they hatch as caterpillars to eat the emerging leaves and buds. A barrier of grease stops her.

Organic pesticides

If you look at your plants regularly, you will spot pests and diseases before they can get a real grip and can take appropriate action – for instance, in the case of aphids, by simply rubbing them off the plant with your fingers as already explained. If, however, you find that they have become too numerous for this, a blast with the hose will remove most of them, though you shouldn't do it too often as it can destroy beneficial insects as well. Soft soap or the slightly stronger insecticidal soap is the best bet against blackfly, greenfly, whitefly and woolly aphid (these are covered in white fluff, hence the common name) and red spider mite. It destroys the waxy coating that protects their bodies, but does not harm beneficial insects like ladybirds, hoverflies and lacewings. It is a contact insecticide only, killing just the insects it actually touches, and there is no residual effect. If the pests come back, you will have to spray again.

> ❛ *Any rough-textured mulch spread around the plant will help keep the surface crawlers away* ❜

Although derris and pyrethrum are derived from the roots of plants, they are potent insecticides and should be used with great care since they will kill beneficial insects as well as the bad guys. If you must use them, do so late in the evening when insects like bees, hoverflies and lacewings are no longer flying around. Just because they are 'natural' doesn't mean they are safe, of course. If you spray food crops with derris, for example, you should wait at least twenty-four hours before harvesting and eating, and keep it well away from ponds as it is toxic to fish.

Non-organic pesticides

There is a wide range of pesticides on the market, aimed at different pests, but again spray only as a last resort, and do it in the evening. For aphids on ornamental plants, choose a systemic insecticide ('systemic' means it is absorbed into the sap and so will go on poisoning sap-sucking pests for some weeks) containing pirimicarb which will kill only aphids, and, sadly, hoverfly larvae, though it won't affect adult hoverflies, lacewings or ladybirds. For edible crops, carefully check the waiting time between spraying and harvesting and always wash *all* crops whether they are to be cooked or eaten raw.

To control slugs and snails, try mechanical barriers first and only as a last resort use liquid slugkiller or pellets scattered very sparingly around vulnerable plants. They are harmful to other forms of wildlife, not just because other creatures may eat the pellets too (laying pieces of tile on top of the pellets can help here) but because birds such as thrushes eat the poisoned slugs and snails. As with all chemicals, keep them safely locked away from children and pets, and never store pesticides in anything other than their original containers.

Biological controls

There are many organically acceptable biological controls on the market now, most of them for use in greenhouses, though there are some that are valuable in the garden.

A useful biological control against caterpillars is BT 4000, which is based on a bacterium, *Bacillus thuringiensis*, which is bought as a dry powder, mixed with water and sprayed on to the caterpillars. It attacks their digestive system, so that they stop feeding at once and eventually die. It does no harm at all to plants or other creatures, and those killed by it can be safely eaten by birds and other predators.

For a serious slug problem, you can use parasitic nematodes which burrow into the bodies of the slugs, lay their eggs and kill the slugs from the inside. You can buy these in most garden centres now – or rather you pay for them there, then send off the card you are given and they are posted to you by return. You mix them with water and then apply the mixture to the soil with a watering can. There is also another nematode which attacks the larvae of vine weevils, probably the most serious pest for container plants.

For codling moth, another pest of apples, and plum sawfly, an effective method of contol is pheromone traps. These are stout cardboard tents, sticky on the inside, containing the female sex pheromone. Males are lured into the traps where they stick, and so fewer females are fertilized and fewer eggs laid.

Mildew

In organic gardens, Bordeaux mixture, a blend of copper sulphate and slaked lime, can be used against fungus diseases such as potato blight and mildew. It won't cure growth already infected but can protect new growth for a couple of weeks. A home-made spray made from elder leaves simmered in water for half an hour is also said to be effective against mildew. You need 450g (1lb) elder leaves to 3.5 litres (6 pints) of water and you must keep the water regularly topped up to the original level. Once it is cool, strain it and keep it in bottles. It should last for three months or so. It is also said to kill aphids, but will not harm ladybirds or their larvae.

Non-organic gardeners use Bordeaux mixture too, but they can also use fungicides based on benomyl, or bupirimate and triforine.

INDEX